China 1- United States and Its Allies 0

China 1- United States and Its Allies 0

HOW THE UNITED STATES
AND ITS ALLIES ARE LOSING
THE SOUTH CHINA SEA

———

James M. Fones, CDR USN (Ret.)

ISBN: 1530271738
ISBN 13: 9781530271733
Library of Congress Control Number: 2016903499
CreateSpace Independent Publishing Platform
North Charleston, South Carolina

Table of Contents

Introduction

————

ADMIRAL ISOROKU YAMAMOTO NEVER ACTUALLY said that in attacking Pearl Harbor Japan had done nothing more than awaken a sleeping giant and fill it with a terrible resolve. On the other hand, historians believe this is how he actually felt, and attributing this statement to him does seem to reflect his opinion that the United States was a giant that was sleeping.

This book addresses why the American giant should once again be awakened so it may defend itself and protect our interests and the interests of the littoral (coastal) nations that border the South China Sea and around the world against unjust and illegal Chinese expansion supported by Russia.

President Barack Hussein Obama and his executive branch of our government have followed and continue to follow the failed tactic of appeasement when dealing with China and Russia. Nothing has been done by all administrations since the beginning of Chinese aggression in the South China Sea (1974) to awaken the sleeping American giant. Therefore, our submission to the will and political conquest of the South China Sea formations by the People's Republic of China continues daily.

An analysis will be provided herein on the effects of appeasing China, no matter how gross its aggression against our allies, by studying China's behavior over the last century and intentionally ignoring any verbiage put forward by China's leadership. The analysis will focus on the premise that a country's behavior, like that of humans, is more indicative of its true intent rather than written and spoken words issued by leaders. There will also be an attempt to integrate China's behavioral patterns as related to the world stage and specific moments and events that preceded major changes in China's foreign policy.

During the Obama administration, the Russians and Chinese appear to have had and are having a great impact on the increased aggressiveness as related to its island (territorial) disputes with Japan and the littoral nations of the South China Sea.

The People's Republic of China appears to be relying on two principles that are not accepted when viewed through the prism of international law. For example, the Chinese leadership keeps referring to history and use of the formations in the South China Sea for hundreds of years. Additionally, they keep bringing up the Nine-Dashed-Line Map created in 1933 as evidence that the entire South China Sea and all the formations and water areas within its territorial seas are theirs.

Another line of reasoning China takes when attempting to bolster its right to possess the entire South China Sea is that no regulatory body, such as the United Nations, has the right to act as an arbiter of the disputes with its neighbors. If one of the littoral nations insists on its right to freely use areas of the South China Sea, China claims the United Nations, United States, and any third country should stay out of the dispute between China and its neighbors, notwithstanding the United Nations Law of the Sea III (UNCLOS III) ratified by China. China continually claims UNCLOS III supports its position to exercise sovereignty over the South China Sea formations and its waters.

To further cloud the issues, China, without openly declaring that the formations in the South China Sea are islands, continues to build structures and increases the area size of the rock formations and islets in an apparent attempt to classify them in the future as Article 121(3) islands. If the littoral nations, the United States, and the United Nations allow China to classify these formations as islands, it may then claim a two-hundred-nautical-mile exclusive economic zone (EEZ) using the quasi-islands' baseline as the nexus of the zone.

China also seems to analyze the political climate of the United States (the giant) prior to increasing or changing its strategy and its prosecution of aggressively taking over areas of the South China Sea. A correlation will be shown between periods when the giant is sleeping, distracted by politics or recovering from wounds previously received in world battles, with increases in China's aggressive behavior supporting the spread of humans subjected to communist domination and socialist economic domination.

Finally, a detailed analysis of the formations using the International Law of the Sea and its provisions for litigating disputes between nations, and the definition of what constitutes an "island" will be explored. There are many excellent studies that provide a legal basis for China's claim not surviving adjudication before any legitimate body; this book will reiterate the findings of many outstanding papers written by eminent scholars and rely on their findings in an attempt to help readers understand what is motivating China to be so bold by intentionally ignoring international law. And, as mentioned previously, I will attempt to analyze why the sleeping giant remains comatose while being attacked from three distinct belligerent forces: the People's Republic of China, Russia, and militant Islamic organizations. And then I discuss what must be done.

CHAPTER 1

Judging China by Its Actions (History)

———

PRIOR TO THE TWENTIETH CENTURY, China was subjected to many injustices at the hands of more organized and powerful nations of the world. She suffered from internal conflicts between various powerful warlords and organizations. Starting with many factional leaders' attempts to organize China after the fall of the last emperor, two major political divisions became apparent— the nationalist and the communist/socialist. The communist and socialist group won but only with the help of the Soviet Union.

Once mainland China was consolidated under communist leadership after WWII, it started to expand its territory using the Marx/Lenin concepts of world domination. For reasons discussed in this writing, the free world was never successful in helping the Chinese people live free. History is a great teacher, and by reviewing China's and Russia's past actions, perhaps their future aggressive behavior and noncompliance with appeasement and international law can be predicted.

WAR OF 1812—JAMES MADISON

Prior to the start of the war with Great Britain in 1812 Britain was at war with France. (Napoleonic Wars) America was neutral during this war and continued trading with both France and Great Britain. The British navy continually disrupted this trade at the expense of American businesses and shipping. The disruption went so far as British war ships impressing American merchant sailors to serve on British war ships. Three impressed Americans escaped their

British captures and made their way on board the U.S.S. Chesapeake. The U.S. refused to return the sailors to the British which led to the issuance of orders to all British ship sighting the Chesapeake to deliver an order from the British Admiralty to return the sailors. In due course the H.M.S. Leopard cross paths with the Chesapeake and after coming alongside delivered the Admiralty's demand to Captain James Barron, USN. Captain Barron refused to deliver the men so the Leopard pushed off and took the Chesapeake under fire. The Chesapeake, a frigate, was severely out gunned by the Leopard (50 to 38) and was damaged by Leopard's first volley. Captain Barron was forced to surrender four sailors, one British and three American citizens. The British sailor was hanged for treason and the three Americans were eventually returned to the United States. This action by Great Britain was one of the major causes leading to the War of 1812.

As a direct result of Great Britain's action the Madison government changed the worldwide embargo to focus only on France and Great Britain. Through the Nonintercourse Act, Congress, realizing hostilities were not abating, passed Macon's Bill No. 2, which offered a settlement agreement to both France and Great Britain. The first nation to repeal its restrictions on neutral shipping would be favored economically by a Nonintercourse Act staying in force against all other nations. Napoleon gave in first, and Great Britain was left as the only nation being antagonistic toward the United States. The French did not honor their agreement and continued seizing American ships.

An analogy can be drawn between Great Britain's postindependence behavior and that of North Vietnam after the Geneva Accords. Both nations continued to fight using external forces. North Vietnam used the Russians and Chinese, and Great Britain used Canadians and Native Americans. The United States was at a disadvantage militarily because Congress had cut spending on military forces. Notwithstanding this deficiency, the Americans fought Great Britain to a draw, which was ended by the signing of the Treaty of Ghent in December 1814.

Great Britain had wanted to overthrow the republican government of its former colony, but it failed. Twentieth-century Chinese strategists could draw similar lessons about the limits on a remote superpower's capacity to project power along the Asian seaboard. How the United States' first major war figures into Chinese commentary—if at all—is worth watching. Great Britain and France had forced exorbitant insurance rates on American shipping, if insurance could be found at all. Hard pressed by merchants, ship owners, and citizens tired of years of war, the British government joined the Americans at the treaty table in Ghent, Belgium, in late 1814, as noted. In this year Great Britain suffered the loss of nearly four hundred ships to American privateers.

Meanwhile, American privateers (many having switched their base from the Chesapeake to such southern ports as Wilmington, Charleston, or Savannah the previous year) ranged the waters of the world, frequently working together to attack British convoys. *Leo* of Baltimore created an international incident when it captured a prize bearing a statue of the late Queen Louise commissioned by the Prussian government. *Rambler*, of Boston, harassed the British China trade, selling British prizes in Asian markets. American privateers boldly snatched prizes in the Thames estuary and then sold them to laughing former allies of the British. On September 30, 1814, Lloyd's of London reported that two American warships and several privateers had captured 108 British prizes that month.

The lessons learned for Russia, China, and the United States were that the power of a nation must be projected around the world to protect the homeland.

BOXER REBELLION: SIEGE OF FOREIGN LEGATION (NOVEMBER 1899 TO SEPTEMBER 1901)

It all started after the Boxer Rebellion and the siege of the Legation Quarters next to the Imperial Palace in Beijing, where refugees gathered to escape from the Militia United in Righteousness (the Boxers). In June 1900, the Boxers were confident they could not be harmed by Western armament because they were protected by their gods and began attacking the ligation. During the second day of the attack, Empress Dowager Cixi supported the Boxers in hopes of ousting all foreign powers from China with emphasis on religious proselytizers.

Cixi was under the initial impression she was ensuring the survival of her Qing Dynasty. The Boxers (Yihetuan) and the Qing Dynasty were not a unified force and operated independently with the outward impression of fighting for the same cause. Empress Cixi had the secret goal of decimating the Boxers while at the same time removing the threat to her dynasty by foreign powers.

Eleven nations had a stake in the outcome of this Boxer-initiated rebellion, and all were positioned to support the Legation Quarters and their citizens trapped therein. They were Spain, Italy, Belgium, the Netherlands, the United Kingdom, Russia, Japan, France, the United States, Germany, and Austria-Hungary.

The rest of the story has been told many times—the combined forces of eight of the eleven nations (approximately twenty thousand armed troops) liberated the legation; the Empress Dowager Cixi denounced the Boxers and had all the leaders executed and agreed to pay 450 million taels of silver to the eight nations over a period of thirty-nine years ($333 million), China paid 668,661,220 taels of silver on time and with interest. The United States used the majority of its share to educate Chinese students in the United States under the Boxer Indemnity Scholarship Program.

During the aftermath of the liberation of the legation and during the negotiations with the Qing Dynasty Empress, ten of the nations wanted to divide China into pieces, and each nation would add its assigned territory as a protectorate, territory, or colony—China as a nation would cease to exit. The only nation resisting the partition of China was the United States (under William McKinley and John Hay, Republicans). Had the United States allowed the partition of China, it would not exist today, and the Chinese would probably have rebelled continuously against their imperial masters.

The US action protecting the integrity of China surely was noticed by the empress dowager and the subsequent Chinese readers of history. In the early 1900s, the United States was sufficiently respected to back down the combined Western nations of the world. Generally, this view of the siege of the legation in Beijing is not discussed, but the important issue is the Chinese leaders have long-term memories and keep constant touch with the past behavior of nations. The United States must now return to its position in the world where other nations of the world respect us enough to back down when the giant so requests.

WORLD WAR I

For the purpose of this analysis, only the actions of nations affecting the United States will be addressed starting with the sinking of the RMS *Lusitania* by German U-boats on May 7, 1915. Following the rhetoric and political position in the United States vehemently condemning the sinking of a nonbelligerent-flagged ship by Germany, Germany reduced the activity of its U-boat fleet in the Atlantic. The US government continued to maintain a political policy of isolationism notwithstanding the sinking of the *Lusitania* with so many American citizens on board.

Germany must have noticed the United States' pacifist stance in reference to the war in Europe and its lack of military response to the sinking of the *Lusitania* and the killing of American citizens. In the spring of 1917, Germany once again and with more aggression started sinking ships of all nations delivering goods to Great Britain and its allies.

In response to the unbridled carnage wrought by Germany, the United States declared war on Germany on April 6, 1917. The United States' entry into the war helped the Allies defeat the Germans, and an armistice was signed on November 11, 1918. It is important to note that Germany became more aggressive when the United States did not respond to the sinking of its ships. Later in this writing, the reader will notice that the Russians and Chinese did the very same thing and continued doing so for decades.

On the other side of the world during this time, China was undergoing a revolution of its own, which, indirectly, led to its entry and declaration of war on Germany on August 14, 1917. The Manchu Dynasty fell to the revolution of its citizens in 1911. Sun Yat-sen, the leader of the revolution and founder of the Kuomintang (KMT) or Nationalist People's Party, had desires to renew dynasty-style leadership with him as the emperor, but the Chinese military leaders forced Sun to return to a republican form of government. China entered the war to earn a seat at the winners' table and regain control of the Shantung peninsula. The United States, France, and Great Britain decided against China and awarded Japan control of Germany's considerable economic possessions in Shantung, including the port of Tsingtao. Japan did turn over control of Shantung to China in February 1922 as required by the armistice agreement.

The Chinese people noticed with rancor that the Western nations once again decided the fate of China and ruled against their country at the armistice table.[1] Riots followed in Tiananmen Square starting on May 4, 1919. The feelings of the rioters were that foreign nations were still selfish and militaristic, and they were all liars. One year after the Versailles Treaty, China joined forces with Russia and established the Chinese Communist Party under the leadership of Mao Tse-tung and Zhou En-lai along with other former leaders of the anti–Versailles Treaty demonstrations. Twenty-nine years later, the Chinese Communist Party, with the aid of Russia, was in control of mainland China.

The lessons learned by the Chinese from the behavior of the US government were these:

- A nation sinking a British-flagged ship, killing American citizens, will not provoke the United States into military action.
- Massive attacks against American shipping will provoke US military action.
- The United States will vote for a stronger nation (Japan) against a weaker one (China). The American political system allows for major swings in foreign policy from one generation of politicians to the next.

World War II

Chairman Mao was the leader or had a leadership position in China from the formation of the Chinese Communist Party in 1921 until his death in 1976—a reign of fifty-five years. During these years, the Chinese Communist Party

---

1 The reader will notice the same action by the United States and other nations at the armistice meetings of both World War I and World War II with Ho Chi Minh's request for independence from France. Ho subsequently became a lifetime proponent of Lenin's theory of revolution when seeking independence.

and its sister, the Russian Communist Party, continued to learn to predict the behavior of its political rivals (all nations *not* subjected to communist/socialist rule) by observing their behavior in response to national stimuli.

For example, the formation of the Free City of Danzig (*Freie Stadt Danzin*) by the Versailles Treaty allowed Poland a major seaport under the protection of the League of Nations. When the Nazi Party took over the city's government in 1939, the League of Nations did nothing to protect the Free City of Danzig.

China's Communist Party was fostered and supported by the Russians. In 1917, a few years before the Chinese Communist Party was founded, the Bolsheviks, later to be renamed the Communist Party of Russia, commenced revolutionary activities against the Russian party in power.

In 1922 the Bolsheviks succeeded and established the Union of Soviet Socialist Republics (USSR) consisting of fourteen Soviet socialist republics and Russia. This union was dissolved in 1991 after complete failure of the socialist form of economics.

Deng Xiao-ping never held office officially in the Chinese government but was the *de facto* leader from 1978 to the early 1990s. During his tenure, he learned from the economic failure of the USSR and the success of a free-market enterprise from many nations, including the United States. To stay true to the communist teachings of Marx and Lenin, he could not endorse the capitalistic style of economics because it directly contradicted Marxist/Leninist doctrine. So he devised a hybrid system of economics for China referred to as "socialism with Chinese characteristics," "Chinese economic reform," or "socialist market economy."

Apparently Deng realized China would follow Russia to economic destruction if it did not move away from a pure socialist-economic-based system. To better understand and follow the analysis herein, the following definitions are used:

* Communism. No government is required; the people of a nation work without guidance from any central government, and each person contributes to the whole what he/she can, and each person

consumes what he/she needs. All citizens are equal, and class distinction is not required (boss, worker; rich, poor; leader, follower; and so forth). Nothing is owned by anyone; everything is owned by all.

* Socialism. One central government owns everything and provides all services required for its citizens. This includes cradle-to-grave care for all human necessities.
* Capitalism (free-market enterprise). Government exists by the will of the citizens and does not interfere with the free-market economic system. Citizens are free to form organizations for their use by democratic free elections.
* Federalism. A nation consists of independent organizations (states and territories, for example), which agree to be protected by a central government that has the power to raise and maintain military forces, manage the flow of capital (create money), and represent the independent organizations (states) internationally.

With these brief definitions, one can question Deng's rationale behind his quote, "A basic contradiction between socialism and the market economy does not exist."[2] The obvious contradiction is that in a socialistic system, the government owns everything and is responsible for the care and feeding of all citizens. A free-market enterprise cannot exist when the government owns all.

In reference to competing political systems and foreign policy, Deng was more credible. He has been quoted as saying, "The United States brags about its political system, but the President says one thing during the election; something else when he takes office, something else at midterm and something else when he leaves (office)."[3] He could have added that foreign policy varies with political parties, and common sense is not allowed to determine what is best for the federation of states.

With a better understanding of China's leadership positions, we can continue with our analysis of what its leadership probably learned from the period

---

2 *Daily Report: People's Republic of China*, editions 240–249, 1993, 30.
3 *The Pacific Rim and the Western World: Strategic, Economic, and Cultural Perspectives*, 1987, 105.

of political history immediately prior to World War II. For example, the Italian bombardment of the Greek island of Corfu on August 31, 1923, in an attempt to extract money from Greece for the murder of an Italian general in Greece went unnoticed by the world. The League of Nations once again did nothing to protect Italy's neighbors from the fascist leader Benito Mussolini.

China, once again, was subjected to a foreign nation's unjustified aggression without the League of Nations or the United States helping to stop the warring, attacking nation. Japan attacked China on September 19, 1931, using the false-flag bombing against a Japanese-owned railroad and blaming Chinese dissidents for the attack. The only act by the United States was a proclamation by Secretary of State Henry L. Stimson called the Stimson Doctrine. The doctrine held that the US government would not recognize border changes that were made by force—this is a basic tenet of international law. The Chinese were left on their own to fight off the superior forces of Japan.

The Shanghai violence is addressed in a following section and is one example where the threat of the United Kingdom of Great Britain using its sea power was sufficient to stop the Japanese. Once again the Chinese probably reinforced their understanding that superior military force did not need to exercise its power; sometimes the mere threat of its use is enough. The United States must once again have and maintain a superior military force.

Another lesson China and Russia both learned from World War II was that once the sleeping giant was awakened, it had the capability to amass an overwhelming military presence anywhere in the world. An offshoot of this lesson is that China should never attack the United States directly. As history progressed, it seems China learned that it could poke the giant, and it would grunt but not become fully awake.

SYNOPSIS OF THE CHINA-RUSSIA RELATIONSHIP

The mainstream media generally focus on trade between China and Russia and diplomatic exchanges. Since the Stalin era, these countries have had on-and-off relations. The main cooling period began in the late 1950s and ended in the 1990s. The common bond that is not reported or has never been a major topic of political discussion in the United States is that the Chinese-Russian relationship has always been used to balance the American influence in Asia. The second topic—not a subject of analysis or published in the mainstream media—has been the mutual goal of both countries to eliminate the democratic free-market capitalistic economies of various countries, especially the United States.

The goal of both Russia and China is to weaken the United States politically and create internal strife and class warfare. By so doing, the way is paved for Russia and China to establish communist/socialist US governments open to accepting the Chinese-Russian-style totalitarian governments.

The focus of this book is the South China Sea and how the United States and its allies are losing control of this vital ocean highway to the Chinese. The long-term venture by the People's Republic of China (PRC) has been going on since the 1970s and will not stop until the Communist Party of China has control of the entire sea. This acquisition is nothing but a stepping-stone to gaining complete control of the world.

One issue the Chinese need to solve is how to increase the well-being of its citizens by improving their diet. Russia has excess capacity for food production, and China has trouble feeding its 1.4 billion citizens. Table 1 will help readers understand the impossibility of China feeding its citizens without outside supplies of food.

Table 1. Comparison of Countries to the United States; Acres of Cultivation per Citizen

Country	Agricultural Land Km² Available	Percentage under Cultivation	Area under Cultivation Km²	Population	Acres of Cultivated Land for One Citizen
Russia	1.2×10^6	13.1%	157×10^3	0.14×10^9	0.28
China	1.5×10^6	54.8%	822×10^3	1.40×10^9	0.14
United States	1.7×10^6	44.7%	760×10^3	0.33×10^9	0.57

This table is based on annual statistics; note the United States uses approximately four times as much agricultural land to feed each citizen as China does and approximately two times as much as Russia. True, this table does not take into account multiple variables that affect the amount and quality of food available by these three countries, but it is provided to illustrate China's need to form an alliance with Russia to help feed its people. To emphasize this point, the following excerpt was taken from *The Hueber Report*, written by Dan Hueber for the AgWeb and Farm Journal Media in 2015:

> I did come across an interesting story this morning that twenty years ago would have been unimaginable. It was announced that China and Russia are ready to launch a joint $2 billion agricultural investment fund and set up a free trade zone between the two countries. Needless to say, China needs to continue securing a reliable supply of food for its 1.36 billion population and Russia is trying to expand agricultural production/exports and of course needs friends. This would appear to be another prime example of how many nations outside of the United States continue to pour investments into agriculture to secure food needs for the future.[4]

The alliance between Russia and China is mutually beneficial and is no cause for concern. On the other hand, if Russia and China are forming this and other alliances to cut out importing food products from the United States, then there is reason to be concerned. In 2014 the United States exported approximately $29.9 billion of agricultural products. What if China shifted its needs from the United States to Russia based on the new alliance? The American industries listed in Table 2 would probably collapse.[5]

---

4   Dan Hueber, *The Hueber Report*, May 8, 2015, retrieved from www.agweb.com/blog/ the-huber-report/china-russia-alliance/.

5   USDA Global Agricultural Trade System database—2013; retrieved from http://www.fas. usda.gov/search/2013.

Table 2. Industries in Danger of Collapse if Trade with Russia Is Interrupted

Product	Quantity
Pork	175,000 metric tons
Soy	25,000,000 metric tons
Corn	5,000,000 metric tons
Nuts—Walnuts	27,000 metric tons
Nuts—Almonds	25,000 metric tons
Nuts—Pistachios	10,000 metric tons
Alfalfa	600,000 metric tons
Wine	18,000 liters

The total exports to China reported by the Department of Agriculture amounted to approximately 20 percent of America's products. On the other hand, the United States could cut off export to China to control their political behavior. Doing this would definitely cause economic issues in the United States, but at some time in the future, a decision will have to be made whether to commit our military or use economic pressure to protect the well-being of the United States from Chinese-Russian aggression.

To understand what the Russian-Chinese end game is, we should understand the history of the on-off relationship between these countries.

1894–1937: Shaking Off Dynastic Rule

The Chinese empire came to an end in 1906, and a struggling form of constitutional government attempted to survive and organize numerous factions vying to take the place of the last emperor, Pu Yi. Warlords filled the power vacuum, and three leaders commenced developing a political base: Sun Yat-sen, Chiang Kai-shek, and Mao Tse-tung.

Hardly ever reported by the mainstream media is how the Soviets supported these early leaders of China. The Russian Comintern agent known as Borodin helped Sun Yat-sen organize the Communist Party and the Guomindang into the first united front designed to lead all of China down the Marxist/Leninist road of state organization. Chiang Kai-shek and his wife, Soong Qing-ling, were believers in free-market enterprise and capitalism based on observing the growth and development of countries using these economic systems.

Between the 1920s and the early 1930s, Chiang and his allies turned against the communists and started purging them from society. By 1920 Mao Tse-tung described himself as "a Marxist in theory and to some extent in action," and in July of 1921, he was one of a small group that founded the Chinese Communist Party.[6] Mao realized early on that the Marxist/Leninist concept of warfare between the classes would not work in China for the lack of "classes." He therefore set out to mobilize the peasants. Mao was appointed head of the KMT (Kuomintang, or Nationalist Party) Peasant Movement Training Institute. He did believe in the revolutionary potential of the Chinese peasantry, and all his subsequent acts followed this belief.

The year 1927 was pivotal for Mao and his communist followers. In the 1920s Chinese citizens were not aware that the conflict between Trotsky and Stalin would affect the establishment of the Chinese Communist Party. Trotsky supported "Permanent Revolution," and Stalin was a major promoter of "Socialism in One Country." Permanent Revolution has been defined many ways, and for the purpose of showing the connection between Russia and the Communist Party of China, the explanation here will be brief.

The original use of the term by Karl Marx in 1850 may be condensed as follows: "Revolution must continue until all citizens with property have been removed from their ruling positions and the people have taken over state power in all the leading countries of the world."

In other words, take everything from the rich (the haves) and give it to the poor (the have-nots), after which the former have-nots rule the country. Marx

---

6 *Focus on Asian Studies*, vol. IV, no. 1, Fall 1984, New York: The Asia Society.

based this need on his realization that classes only existed in developed countries but were nearly nonexistent in countries such as China. Without large division by economic classes, revolution between the classes was not possible. Marx went on to declare that the revolution must be permanent, consisting of the working class maintaining an independent approach to politics and keeping the proletariat (the have-nots) in power. In 1971 Saul Alinsky published his book *Rules for Radicals* on how to convert democratic free-market-based economic countries to socialism. Hillary Clinton admired Alinsky and became his adopted daughter.

Trotsky was focused on international communism while Stalin was keen on establishing socialism in the Soviet Union—after which socialism could only be developed in other countries with the help of the workers (unions).[7] Trotsky and Stalin in 1926 even argued about when to push the Chinese Communist Party (CCP) to start the revolution of the workers/citizens. Moscow formed the united front with the Guomindang government in Guangzhou (formerly Canton) in 1923. The Comintern (Communist International) provided political, propaganda, and military advisors to China to help develop communism as a central government.

Through these organizations, by 1926 Moscow was able to exert great diplomatic pressure on Beijing, and its goal was to foment nationalist revolution in China that would be anti-imperialist in nature and might lead to ousting all foreigners from China—especially the Japanese from Manchuria. The next goal following the revolution was to establish a socialist revolution under the control of the CCP.

Trotsky wanted to abandon the CCP; Stalin did not. Chiang Kai-shek took power in 1925 and convinced the Guomindang leaders to reunite China militarily using the term "Northern Expedition." Approximately nine warlords were running Northern China and were doing so to enrich their own lives at the expense of the workers. Chiang during this period realized Moscow's

---

7 The discussion of the connection between communism and socialism and its impact on China was made possible by the following references: Bruce Elleman, *Moscow and the Emergence of Communist Power in China, 1925–30: The Nanchang Uprising and the Birth of the Red Army*, Routledge Studies in the Modern History of Asia, 2009; and Chang and Halliday, *Mao: The Unknown Story*, London, 1992, 2004 Perennial edition.

intent on having the Comintern take over China and establish a socialist government. Additionally, he commenced purging communist leaders in 1926 by instigating a political coup and thus reducing the power and influence of Soviet advisors and the Guomindang.

The Northern Expedition was making headway by pushing the communist and warlords out of Nanchang, Hankou, Nanjing, and Shanghai. In early 1927 Chiang led a second cleaning of communists within the Guomindang. The Beijing government also broke relations with Moscow, cleaned out the Soviet embassy, and arrested and executed many important Chinese communists.

Stalin was not a happy socialist. The CCP was being routed in all parts of China, and Trotsky's prediction was coming true. To counter this apparent political coup by Trotsky, Stalin ordered the July 30, 1927, Nanchang uprising to bolster the ideological validity of the socialist Chinese policy. Stalin's intent was to ignite a revolution of the workers of China and overthrow the Nationalist Chinese led by Chiang.

Following Stalin's order, by and through the Comintern, forces (approximately twenty thousand to thirty thousand, depending on source) led by Zhou En-lai supervised by Soviet military advisors captured the city of Nanchang. The nationalist forces ousted the revolutionaries in three days, and the communists retreated in two groups after suffering severe losses during the attack and retreat. Eventually the stragglers united in the Jinggang Shan Mountains for guerrilla warfare training and joined up with Mao. The Chinese celebrate this reunion as the founding of the People's Liberation Army.

The saddest part of this history is that Chinese graduate and undergraduate students have no idea of the influence Stalin had over the Chinese Communist Party. Mao's Long March commenced in 1934, seven years after the Nanchang uprising. During my five years in China, I spoke with over three hundred students and intellectuals. None admitted to knowing about the Soviet influence on the Communist Party in China. Nor were they aware that Russian Agent Otto Braun worked with Mao as an advisor. Braun's strategy was poor and eventually cost the Chinese communists' army many casualties. China has revised its history, which does not represent actual events of the Nanchang uprising. The following is but one example:

After the massacre of communists in Shanghai and elsewhere in 1927 at the instigation of Chiang Kai-shek, the communists attempted rebellions in several cities and towns. The Jiangxi Soviet emerged as a result of attempted insurrections in two cities, an unsuccessful one organized by Mao Tse-tung and a successful one organized by Chou En-lai.

In July of 1927 Chou En-lai journeyed to the city of Nanchang to carry out his assignment by the Central Committee of the Communist Party of China, which was to capture and control Nanchang. Nanchang was chosen because the Guomindang commander of public safety, Zhu De, was secretly a member of the Communist Party. The insurrectionists had about twenty thousand troops, and the troops who remained loyal to Chiang Kai-shek numbered only ten thousand.

The Comintern representative ordered Chou En-lai not to carry out the insurrection. Chou En-lai defied that order even though it might mean a loss of the material support for the Chinese communists by the Soviet Union.

The insurrection was successful. However, it was recognized that once the government (Nationalist) moved substantial numbers of troops to the area, the insurrectionists would not be able to hold the city. The insurrectionists left Nanchang and headed south.

While the nationalists under Chiang were ousting the warlords from Northern China and the Chinese Communist Party was being purged and chased from southern China to the west and then north of China (The Long March—1934–1935), Japan apparently determined it was time to flex its muscle and acquire territory in Manchuria.

1937–1945: Second Sino-Japanese War

Prior to the Sino-Japanese Wars, China suffered continually at the hands of foreign nations; there is no question China was mistreated as a nation during its consolidation. It appears that China learned the lesson that a strong military was necessary to protect the nation from other states that wanted to dominate it. Had it not been for the US intervention at the end of the Boxer Rebellion, China would have been divided into eight or nine foreign territories as noted previously when analyzing the Boxer Rebellion.

Another revision of history taught the Chinese how the Japanese became entrenched in Eastern China. During the First World War, China took the side of France, Great Britain, and Japan under the leadership of its premier, Duan Qi-rui (also Tuan Ch'i-jui), and he sought major loans from Japan for the purpose of supporting the Chinese war effort against Germany. Premier Duan did not use the funds for the war effort; instead he improved and fortified his northern military bases and directed his armies to advance deeper into southern China for the purpose of unifying China under his leadership. A significant portion of the funds were also used to support the political aims of the Anfu Club, a political wing loyal to Duan (literally, Peace and Happiness Club), by financing the purchase of parliamentary and senate seats for Duan supporters.[8]

Premier Duan had to give the Japanese something for their loan, and what he gave up allowed the Japanese to invade China later in the century under the pretext of protecting the Japanese national interest. The following list includes the majority of the concessions granted by China to Japan:

* Extensive rights to develop railways in China
* Extensive rights to develop telecommunications systems in China
* Special concessions in
  * Banking
  * Mining
  * Sales of Japanese military equipment to China

---

8 Twitchett Fairbank, *The Cambridge History of China: Republican China*, 1912–1949, pt. 1, Cambridge University Press, 1978.

Premier Duan, in 1918 and in the name of China, requested and was given another loan from Japan; in return, Japan received the following:

- Special rights in the formerly German-dominated area of Shandong, which the Japanese had occupied since 1914
- Special rights of the formerly German-dominated area of Inner Mongolia, which the Japanese had occupied since 1914
- Japanese rights to station troops in Manchuria
- Japanese rights to station troops in Inner Mongolia
- Contracts to hire Japanese military instructors and advisors to train Duan's forces

Duan's improper use of the loan funds came to the public's attention during the Versailles Treaty negotiations; the Chinese delegation was embarrassed to the point of not signing the treaty. The Chinese people also provided antigovernment sentiment resulting in the May 4, 1919, movement and riots in front of the Tiananmen Gate.

The communist movement in China was greatly augmented by approximately one hundred thousand Chinese who were partially educated by Chinese volunteers who had previously studied in the United States and France. Approximately a thousand student volunteers came from China having been radicalized by the events of May Fourth and the burgeoning Marxist study groups. When the survivors—approximately ninety-eight thousand communist-indoctrinated young men having studied reading, writing, and industrial skills—returned to China, they became active members of the Communist Party of China headed by Li Li-san. By themselves, these returnees would probably not have been able to develop the Communist Party in China, but the Soviet Comintern agents did by infiltrating Peking University and establishing Marxist study groups throughout China.

Sun Yat-sen was also influenced by the Japanese socialist government and the Comintern agents supporting him in his attempts to unify China under a socialist government. The Soviets supported Sun with money, arms, and military advisors for the purpose of ending special privileges for foreigners, especially those granted by his predecessor, Duan Qi-rui, to the Japanese. The Japanese were so well entrenched in Manchuria and Eastern China that the leaders of the Chinese Communist Party (CCP) and Chiang Kai-shek came together to fight the Japanese.

The beginning of the hostilities between Russia and Japan could be traced back to the 1904–1905 Sino-Japanese War, which took place in China. The mainland battles were at Port Arthur, Liaoyang, Mukden, and Shahe. The major sea encounter was off the coast of Korea and named the Battle of Tsushima, and the Japanese attacked Port Arthur and Inchon. By 1939 the Japanese had ousted the Russians and Chinese from

* Manchukuo;
* Mengjiang;
* eastern China, including Peking (Beijing);
* six extensive beachheads, including Macao, Hong Kong, and Shanghai;
* Taiwan;
* Korea; and
* the islands of Ryukyu, the Okinawa chain, the Marianas, the Carolines, the Marshalls, Marcus, Iwo Jima, Bonin, the southern half of Sakhalin Island, and the island chain extending from the Kamchatka peninsula.

These Japanese victories allowed consolidation of its hold on China and surrounding countries. While the alliance between Chiang and the Communist Party of China (CCP) was unholy, it was necessary. Stalin even helped the alliance by directly ensuring Chiang lived after Zhang Xue-liang negotiated a separate peace, against Chiang's orders, with the CCP for the purpose of forming the alliance. Zhang even had his troops launch a surprise attack on Chiang's bodyguards and captured him. Some CCP leaders wanted to kill Chiang, but they were dissuaded by Stalin who believed the time was ripe for a new national united front against Japan's aggression, and Chiang would be a capable leader of the action.[9]

Japan helped push Chiang and the CCP by attacking a Mongolian cavalry unit and retrieving some stray horses that wandered into the Manchukuo area claimed by both Russia and China (May 11, 1939). This incident is referred to as the Nomonhan Incident. After the battles were fought, Russia decisively defeated the Japanese and Manchukuo armies. General Georgy Zhukov was first recognized as a Hero of the Soviet Union, and he gained combat experience that served him well when he defended Moscow against the Germans and had a leading role in the Battle of Stalingrad.

The Japanese never again attacked the Russians and learned not to attack without using small forces to attack over an extended period of time. The Japanese Imperial Command called off a planned strategic offensive to conquer Siberia and support Japan's war efforts.

The alliance did not function smoothly since Chiang had grown to distrust the Soviet advisors, and cooperation started to disintegrate in the late 1930s. By 1940 Soviet influence was wavering, and the CCP troops started to ignore Chiang's orders. In January 1941 Chiang's forces killed at least three thousand communist troops in a series of ambushes and arrested and executed more. The war against Japan was giving way once more to Chinese-against-Chinese hostilities. The alliance between Chiang and the CCP continued in name only, still focusing on the common enemy, Japan.

The Soviets were always lurking in the background, helping the CCP continue its education of the Chinese and rewriting Mao's biography and accomplishments to suit the communist needs. During World War II, there were two separate dramas taking place. The US efforts to help Chiang become an effective leader of his Guomindang forces were fraught with difficulties generally created by Chiang himself. The United States accepted China as a world power with Chiang as its leader and constituted the China-Burma-India theater of operations under General Joseph W. Stilwell, who also served as Chief of Staff for Generalissimo Chiang Kai-shek. The other party to the

---

9 Jonathan D. Spence & Annping Chin, *The Chinese Century*, Random House, New York, 1996.

alliance was the Chinese Communist Party led by Zhou En-lai, Mao Tse-tung, and Zhu De.

Chiang Kai-shek did not fare well as a military leader during the fight against the Japanese and the CCP. General Stilwell's opinion of his capability was very poor. To paraphrase the general's thoughts, Chiang was a microman-ager who based decisions on fragments of intelligence using ill-conceived psy-chology. In addition to his deficient leadership and management abilities, he surrounded himself with swarms of parasites and sycophants. General Stilwell did manage to accomplish one of his goals, and that was to train small num-bers of elite Chinese divisions under the best Chinese officers. These men did well and lived up to General Stilwell's and other Western leaders' opinions that the Chinese would make excellent combatants when well led, armed, and trained.

Chiang's major military blunder in the opinion of this writer was his ignoring French intelligence of the Japanese operation titled "Ichigo." As a result the Japanese dominated in three major battles, killed over five hun-dred thousand Chinese, and overran three provinces. As a result of Chiang's failure, Roosevelt authorized General Stilwell to demand complete control of the Nationalist army. Unfortunately, Stilwell was very rude in passing on President Roosevelt's request, and eventually Stilwell was fired at the insis-tence of Chiang. Many pundits argue that Chiang was more concerned with the CCP than with the Japanese; it turns out he may have been right to worry about the CCP.

Chiang also did not fare well as the head of the Chinese government when he was present at the 1943 meeting with Churchill and Roosevelt in Cairo to decide the future direction of the war. Chiang was ignored, and without his knowledge, Churchill and Roosevelt promised Stalin return of the base at Port Arthur and renewed control over the former Russian railways in Manchuria after the defeat of Japan. This was done to obtain Stalin's agreement to open and prosecute the eastern front to help reduce German pressure against the projected 1944 allied landings in Europe.

On the other hand, at the beginning of the alliance, Zhou and Mao had to regroup after severe losses to the nationalists before and after the

Long March. The CCP leadership felt free to resume a more active program of land reform (take from the haves and give to the have-nots), social control (eliminate dissenters and detractors of communism and socialism), and mass mobilization.

In order to arm and feed their new conscripts, the communist force's highest priority was to harass the Japanese and capture supplies and munitions. Outwardly the focus of the CCP was to push Japan out of China and quietly, with the help of the Soviets, increase Mao Tse-tung's personal power, curb the independence of the intellectuals, and deepen class warfare by identifying class enemies. In order to provide Mao impeccable credentials to lead the CCP, Mao's and the party's history was rewritten to ensure compliance with the "correct" line of thoughts and actions leading to the class of "poor peasantry" of China, which would be mobilized for revolution against the landlords and the rich peasants. Mao's new history was based on his in-depth reading of Marxist philosophy and his simple lifestyle in Yanan living in caves and guerrilla fighting.

The previous descriptions of bits and pieces of the Second Sino-Japanese War provide the necessary information to support a thesis on the relationship between China and Russia leading up to the abrupt end of the war with the surrender of Japan. On August 8, 1945, at 1100 hours Trans-Baikal time, the Soviets informed Japanese Ambassador Sato that the Soviet Union had declared war on the empire of Japan, and beginning on August 9, 1945, the Soviet government would consider itself to be at war with Japan. Russia invaded Manchuria at one minute past midnight on August 9, and they did not stop at the area previously identified with the Manchus (Manchuria). Generalissimo Chiang Kai-shek now faced the Chinese Communist Party and Soviet control of Northern China.

The Russians got away with the deception because the United States did not want to anger the Soviet bear by denying them their land grab from the Japanese, which the Soviets had accomplished merely by declaring war against Japan just days after the atomic bombing of Hiroshima on August 6, 1945.

1945–1960s: The CCP, the KMT, Russia, Tibet, Korea, and the Soviet-CCP Split

Several theories exist as to why the Soviets returned Manchuria and other Chinese territories voluntarily, and it would not serve the purpose of this book to analyze these reasons in depth. The most logical explanation was the Russians had just concluded a horrendous war and suffered an estimated twenty million dead. They were probably aware of the Chinese guerilla warfare capability, and Stalin was not interested in continued fighting to maintain a territory with a very dense Chinese population. Stalin was, however, interested in continuing world domination following the Marx/Lenin Manifesto. What Stalin did order was the dismantling of all industry in the occupied territory and moved the spoils of war to the Soviet Union.

From 1945 to approximately 1965, the Soviet Union supported China and the Chinese Communist Party. With the exception of stripping Northern China (Manchuria) of all its industrial plants and infrastructure, the Soviets provided designs, equipment, and skilled labor to help rebuild and modernize the PRC.

The Chinese noticed quickly that the promises of the Soviets did not match delivery. Perhaps the change in Soviet leadership had an impact on the relations with the PRC. Stalin died on March 5, 1953. He was worshiped by many as the savior of Soviet Russia notwithstanding the ten million plus citizens who were killed at his behest. He was followed by Georgy Malenkov but in name only. Nikita Khrushchev effectively dominated Soviet foreign policy until 1964 as the chairman of the Council of Ministers. During this period of Russia-PRC support, Mao, depending on Soviet support and even permission of Soviet leadership, invaded Tibet and Korea.

Tibet

In 1949 and 1950, China decided to increase communist influence over the independent nation of Tibet, claiming that it was a part of China and always had been. The geopolitical equivalent would be Great Britain taking over the

United States, claiming that a onetime possession means any state can take territory if at one time in history it had a possessory interest in that territory. Following the Chinese interpretation of geopolitics, Spain would have a right to Florida, Mexico, and Texas.

The issue presented by Mao's claim can only be resolved by looking at the history of the country. The Chinese in 1949 chose only to go back as far as necessary to support their claim of "indisputable sovereignty" over Tibet because it had always been a part of China. If one uses common sense and goes back to the beginning of time, a different story unfolds.

Tibet was initially inhabited approximately twelve thousand to eleven thousand years ago and over time was the focus of ancient trade routes from India, China, and Central Asia. Tibet emerged in history as an ethnic group in the seventh century CE as an independent kingdom with its capital at Lhasa. The tenth century was a turbulent time for Tibet because the Tang Dynasty conducted many campaigns and attempts to take over the country and destroy Tibet Buddhism.

The Mongols, using brute force, conquered Tibet, and its leader, Kublai Khan—emperor of China—was converted to Buddhism by the abbot of Sakya Lamasery; the abbot returned to Tibet with Kublai Khan's blessings, establishing the Sakya Dynasty and becoming the first llama to rule Tibet, similar to the Vatican for Catholics. In 1720 the Ch'ing Dynasty replaced Mongol rule in China and Tibet, and this is the event on which the Chinese claim sovereignty, though it was in name only because China did not exercise administrative control of Tibet.

During the eighteenth century during British rule of India, the Gurkha invaded Tibet and brought an end to peace and rapprochement with Britain and China. The Gurkha are not an "ethnic group," but all Gurkhas come mainly from the Limbu, Rai, Gurung, and Magar people of Nepal. Therefore, following the Chinese analysis of geopolitics, Great Britain has rights to Tibet superior or equal to those of the Mongolians or Han Chinese.

Throughout the nineteenth century, Tibet maintained its traditional seclusion and avoided all contact with the British and Chinese. The British, possibly believing they had a right to trade where they wanted in Tibet based on the Gurkha invasion, sent a military expedition in 1904 led by Sir Francis Younghusband to Lhasa, forcing the Tibetans to allow British trading posts in three different parts of Tibet. Great Britain decided that China should be the sovereign over Tibet without Tibetan consent. The geopolitical event of significance before Mao's invasion was in 1912 when the Tibetans ousted the Chinese from Tibet and lived in peace and seclusion until the Chinese invasion in 1949.

Once China dominated Tibet militarily, it commenced its normal procedure of forcing the Tibetan population to comply with communist-socialist political and economic policies. Tibet's leaders reached out to the world for help to fend off the Chinese aggression, but none came. China ignored all UN resolutions condemning China's violations of human rights in Tibet and calling upon China to respect those rights, including Tibet's right to self-determination. The American giant was busy elsewhere in the world and chose not to intervene in the destruction of this independent country.

The Soviet Union did come to the aid of its communist partner by providing Soviet aircraft and munitions used in bombing monasteries and supporting other Chinese punitive operations in 1959 when Tibetans tried to take their country back. The Chinese eventually destroyed over six thousand monasteries between 1959 and 1961; all remnants of Tibetan Buddhism and educational institutions were replaced by secular curricula. The 1959 rebellion was not the last major effort by Tibetans to regain control of their country. In 2008 they tried again, and the brutality and human-rights abuses by China are well documented elsewhere.

It is difficult to piece together the number of humans murdered by the Chinese to gain control of Tibet, so estimates will have to do. To arrive at an estimate of how many Tibetans lost their lives to China's elimination of Tibetans' freedom of thought, religion, and culture may be done using Chinese census as the basis for a crude analysis provided in the following table.

Table 3. Statistics for Calculating Tibetans Killed by Chinese[10]

Year	Ethnic Tibetan Population in Tibet – Census: Dailai Lama (Dashag Government)	Ethnic Tibetan Population in Tibet – Census: Chinese Administration	Projected Tibetan Annual Growth Rate Using 2.25% per annum Based on Medium Growth Rate of Tibetans Residing in China; 1950 Population x Growth Rate
1950	1,270,000	1,150,000	1,640,000/1,490,000
1964	1,210,000	1,350,000	1,560,000/1,740,000
2010	2,090,000	Unknown	----------------------

Assuming a growth rate provided by China of 0.025% per annum and using the 1950 Chinese census of 1,150,000 then the population of Tibetans in Tibet should have been approximately 3,000,000. The question then becomes what happened to the 1,000,000 Tibetans no longer residing in Tibet? The Chinese propaganda machine is claiming that conditions have improved for the Tibetans because of the Communist Party of China's benevolent treatment of the ethnic Tibetans. Even dividing the estimate by two still leaves over half a million Tibetans unaccounted for. Perhaps the Tibetan estimate that 430,000 Tibetans killed during the 1959 uprising seems more accurate than the Chinese's admitted number of 87,000.

It must be remembered that Mao's Great Leap Forward (1959–1962) caused between 18 and 32.5 million deaths in China; these numbers put the estimated Tibetan deaths in perspective. All these deaths were caused by the Communist Party of China trying to control human nature's desire to be free and live peacefully without government interference.

---

10 For a detailed research paper on this subject see *Tibetan Population, Inside and Outside Tibet*, May 2015, Toronto, found at https://tibetdata.gitub.io/projects/population/index.html

Visiting professors in China are not allowed to address, discuss, or even mention "Tibet." The reason given by the Chinese government is if Tibet is mentioned, it would be disruptive to good order and discipline. Students in my classes did, however, with very little encouragement parrot the party line: Tibet was and always had been a province of China, and China had a right to invade and reestablish its control.

I assigned a project (without mentioning Tibet or any country) requiring research papers on how one can recognize a state. The key elements identified by the students in no particular order were an individual flag; administrative control of the state by a central government; common language, customs, and traditions; recognition by other states; and diplomatic exchanges.

Even when confronted with facts that Tibet had all the trappings and behaviors of an independent country, the Chinese university students still believed that the relatively brief period of foreign domination over Tibet occurring seven hundred years ago by the Yuan emperor was sufficient evidence that Tibet was always a Chinese province. To further complicate dealings with China are several generations of Chinese who have been indoctrinated prior to reaching puberty that all Westerners lie and the Chinese Communist Party and its teachings are always true.

KOREA

At the end of World War II, Stalin forced his interpretation of communism on Bulgaria, Czechoslovakia, East Germany, Poland, Hungary, Romania, Yugoslavia, and Albania. In reference to China, in the early days of the Soviet Union around the time of the Russian civil war, the Soviet Union created a new Soviet Mongolian client state, which in 1924 became the People's Republic of Mongolia. During the same time frame, between 1921 and 1926, the Soviet Union supported the Kuomintang (KMT) based on a treaty signed between the Communist Party of China as instructed by the Russian Communist Party with the KMT.

The Chinese civil war between Chiang Kai-shek and Mao Tse-tung started before World War II. The United States and Russia advised the parties to sign the above-mentioned treaty to protect China from the Japanese. Russia had established itself in Manchuria before World War II by occupying it. Mao set up his headquarters in Manchuria with the support of the Russian Communist Party. By 1927 General Chiang separated the Chinese Communist Party from the KMT, which resulted in the beginning of the Chinese civil war, which lasted until 1950.

Russia, after the surrender of Germany and two days after the atomic bombing of Hiroshima, saw an opportunity to advance communism, so it opportunistically entered the war against Japan in Manchuria. After Japan was defeated in China by the Russians, the Soviet Union directed that all weapons captured from the Japanese were to be given to the Communist Party of China (CPC). The Russians continued to support Mao with food, money, arms, and advisors until 1950, when Chiang Kai-shek retreated to Taiwan.

After Mao formed the People's Republic of China, it proclaimed the Soviet Union was its closest ally, and Soviet designs, equipment, and skilled labor were provided to Chairman Mao to help industrialize and modernize his new republic. Mao and Stalin were very strongheaded men, and based on the number of innocent people they murdered, it seems logical they would have their differences of opinion. The relationship between the two was never smooth— Mao from the beginning of their relationship largely ignored Stalin's advice and instructions on how to conduct the revolution in China. Stalin insisted the Chinese revolution should be focused on the urban working class; what he failed to realize was that this class barely existed in China. Mao therefore ignored the traditional communist dogma and sought to mobilize the peasantry.

Notwithstanding the difference of opinion concerning how to implement a communist government, Chairman Mao spent two months in Moscow, and this visit culminated in the Treaty of Friendship and Alliance with Stalin in 1950. Mao had already proclaimed the establishment of the People's Republic of China on October 1, 1949. One year later, with the new treaty in hand and Russian support, Mao invaded Tibet, realizing there was no vast peasantry that he could encourage to revolt against the religious power structure of the Buddhists. With the continuing support and encouragement of the Soviet Union, Mao invaded South Korea twenty-five days later.

There are many similarities between the Korean War and the Vietnam War. The Japanese occupied the Korean peninsula from the Yalu River south from 1910 to 1945. The Soviet Union entered the war against Japan after the atomic bomb attack on Hiroshima when it was obvious that Japan was being defeated. Part of the reward for entering the conflict even at such a late date was that the Soviet Union occupied Korea from the Yalu River border with China to the 38th parallel. The United States occupied the Korean peninsula south of the same parallel. From the division of the Korean peninsula in 1945 until the date of invasion of South Korea on June 25, 1950, over two million Koreans escaped from the Russian-controlled North Korea and relocated to the United States–controlled South Korea.

The North Korean government decided to adopt the Soviet Union and China's communist/socialist doctrine and by 1949 had nationalized 90 percent of the manufacturing capability of North Korea. Additionally, all landowners were stripped of their holdings and either reduced to poverty or assassinated. North Korea had a starting advantage by controlling power generation that was needed by South Korea, but this deficiency was overcome quickly by the South. Also South Korea had the advantage in population—North Korea's population at the time of the invasion was approximately 7.9 million and South Korea was 15.6 million.

Prior to the Korean War, South Korea increased its domestic production between 1946 and 1949 by 250 percent. North Korea's production levels are not known but are believed to have decreased during the same period of time. It must have been obvious to the North Korean leadership that the capitalistic economic system and allowing the South Korean population to be free were more effective than the communistic/socialistic single-party totalitarian government control, which was not working. So with the backing, encouragement, and permission of Stalin and Mao, North Korea invaded South Korea on June 25, 1950.

The consensus of opinion on why North Korea invaded South Korea seems to be a desire to unify the country and control its political future. Russia and China were constantly encouraging Kim Il-sung to spread the communist doctrine throughout Korea and to stop the development of a democratic/

capitalistic system in the South. No other explanation seems to be logical, especially in view of the current developments and political systems in place in North and South Korea.

This brings us to the question of why did China and Russia jointly intervene in the Korean War? It should be noted that by 1948–1949 Russia and the United States had withdrawn the majority of their armed forces from the peninsula. Dr. Jian Chen, holder of the Michael J. Zak Chair of History for US-China Relations at Cornell University concluded Mao's intervention in Korea was not just for the purpose of supporting a communist regime; it was also a method of expanding the Chinese-style revolution to the entire Korean peninsula.[11]

And based on my personal discussions with undergraduate students over a five-year period in China (2003–2008), I discovered they were taught that China was defending its borders from invasion by the United States—in other words, had China not aggressively attacked, the United Nations forces and the United States would have invaded China. It was interesting to learn from students that the Chinese version of history of the intervention does not mention the Soviet Union's support.

In 1949 and 1950, the Soviets continued to arm North Korea, and in April of 1950, Stalin gave Kim permission to invade the South under the condition that Mao would agree to send reinforcements if they became needed. The Soviets made it clear they would avoid a direct confrontation between Soviet troops and the United States.[12] Kim met with Mao in May 1950, and Mao expressed concern the Americans would intervene but agreed to support the North Korean invasion.

Unbiased historians agree China desperately needed the economic and military aid promised by the Soviets to continue even though the Chinese civil war was over and the nationalists had been pushed out of the mainland on December 8, 1949. In the spring of 1950, Mao was in the process of demobilizing half the People's Liberation Army's 5.6 million soldiers, and to help

11   Jian Chen, *China's Road to the Korean War: The Making of the Sino-American Confrontation*, New York: Columbia University Press, 1994.

12   Kathryn Westhersby, *Should We Fear This? Stalin and the Danger of War with America*, Cold War International History Project: Working Paper No. 39, 2002.

North Korea invade South Korea, he sent more ethnic Korean PLA veterans to Korea and promised to move an army closer to the Korean border.

Once Mao and Stalin had completed their commitments, Kim's preparations for war accelerated to take advantage of the departure of the US forces.[13,14] By September of 1949, when the Soviets detonated their first atomic bomb, the Americans had completely withdrawn from South Korea. Stalin, Kim, and Mao must have factored in the American giant not coming to the aid of the nationalists and allowing the spread of communism to the entire mainland of China and the democratic administrations of Roosevelt and Truman allowing the Soviet Union to force communism on a vast majority of Europe.

The North Koreans left unaided by the Soviet Union and China would have had a poorly equipped and trained armed force; their best-trained fighters were the ethnic Koreans returning to their homeland after fighting with the Chinese forces for years. With the aid of China and the Soviets, by 1950 North Korean forces were estimated between 150,000 and 200,000 troops as compared to only 65,000 combat troops and 33,000 in a support role mustered by South Korea. The North also had over 280 tanks (Russian), 150 fighter aircraft (Russian), and over 100 Illyushin II-2 attack bombers (Russian). South Korea did not have an effective air force, and the United States refused to provide tanks as requested by South Korean leaders.

With this imbalance of power, the North pushed the South down the entire Korean peninsula by September of 1950. By the end of September, the South Korean army plus reinforcements from United Nation's forces outnumbered the North Koreans by 180,000 to 100,000, plus the South now had US support of 500 medium tanks battle-ready for the breakout at Pusan. Simultaneously, General of the Armies Douglas MacArthur landed at Inchon (now known as Incheon) close to Seoul.

At this point in the war, on September 18, Stalin sent General H. M. Zakharov to Korea to advise Kim Il-sung to halt his attack on Pusan and redeploy to protect Seoul. China's Zhou En-lai suggested North Korea should

---

13 Ibid.

14 Mark O'Neill, "Soviet Involvement in the Korean War: A New View from the Soviet-Era Archives," *OAH Magazine*.

withdraw to the north if they could not stop the Inchon landing; this they did.

The Soviet Union's involvement in this war was so deep that on September 27, 1950, Stalin convened an emergency session of the Politburo in which the North Korean commanders were judged incompetent and Stalin's Soviet military advisors were held responsible for the defeat. Additionally, China's Zhou En-lai on September 30 warned the United States that China would intervene in Korea if the United States crossed the 38th parallel.

This statement by China must have surprised the world because the Soviet Union was the official occupier of North Korea until its unification, which had not taken place. General MacArthur believed the only strategy to free Korea from communist oppression was to invade China to cut off the flow of armed personnel and logistical support to North Korea. President Truman, representing the sleeping American giant, disagreed and eventually fired General MacArthur.

At the end of World War II, General George S. Patton Jr. and Sir Winston Churchill agreed the American giant should remove the totalitarian government of the Soviet Union (Joseph Stalin), but fear and politics allowed the Soviets to continue to expand their terrorist methods of overcoming the natural human desire for freedom. On October 1, 1950, Stalin had his ambassador forward a telegram to Mao and Zhou requesting China send five to six divisions into Korea, and Kim Il-sung sent frantic appeals to Mao for Chinese intervention. Stalin, once again, emphasized that Soviet forces themselves would not directly intervene. And, as some say, the rest is history.

Chinese and North Koreans today are still being lied to by their totalitarian single-party governments. Generations have been misled by revised history to fit the needs of these communist/socialist governments. Chinese history books cite the number of United Nations forces killed in Korea at over one million; in reality the United States suffered 36,516 dead, which included 2,830 noncombatants; the other nations fighting to preserve freedom in South Korea suffered only 3,125 casualties in total.

In reference to their own casualties, the Chinese and North Koreans were told they only suffered 114,000 combat dead, 21,000 killed by cold weather, and 13,000 by disease. The actual figures are four times higher, with over 400,000 Chinese combat dead, 215,000 North Korean casualties, and 315 Russians. As previously noted, single-party, totalitarian governments cannot be trusted to tell the truth unless it benefits the continued expansion of communism and socialism.

The Republic of Korea (South Korea) had good reason to not want to unify with the Democratic Republic of Korea (North Korea) because of the needs of humans to be free—even when living with an imperfect political system, freedom from totalitarian, single-party governments provides for recognition, earned status, and the right to pursue one's own happiness.

Today, the Democratic Republic of Korea does not report its GNP, and the Republic of Korea is up to $25,920 per year being produced by each free South Korean (GNP/capita).

As noted, the Soviets and Chinese slowly grew apart because of ideological positions on how to force the world's free population to accept communist/socialist ideology. As noted also, Mao, while fighting the Japanese and the nationalists (KMT), ignored advice and recommendations from Stalin and the Comintern because he felt class warfare would not be possible in China for the lack of classes.

The most impressive indicator that Stalin's primary goal was worldwide domination by communists was his breaking his agreement with Generalissimo Chiang and their Treaty of Friendship and Alliance, signed on August 14, 1945, which was to be valid for thirty years. In the treaty, Stalin recognized the nationalists (KMT) as being the only legitimate government of China. Additionally, Stalin recognized that the nationalists were the rightful dominant political power of the territory taken by the Soviets in August of 1945 (Manchuria). Stalin also assured Washington and President Truman that the Soviets would ensure the unification of China under Chiang and the nationalists.

Stalin, within three months of signing the treaty, broke it by giving Manchuria to Mao. To further rub Generalissimo Chiang's and President Truman's noses in mud, Stalin gave Mao weaponry and all the spoils of war from the Imperial Japanese forces. The United States did nothing to counter this gross violation of amity with the Soviets because the American giant was busy with the blockade of Berlin by the Soviets. To further solidify the Soviet/China block, Mao and Stalin concluded the Sino-Soviet Treaty of Friendship and Alliance, which included a thirty-year military alliance and a low-interest loan to China of approximately $300 million.

Cuba

The American giant sometimes finds itself in a quandary over whether to support a ruthless, vengeful, despicable politician or ignore all his faults in the interest of protecting American assets in the subject country. It chose unwisely when faced with this decision in Cuba in the 1940s and 1950s.

Starting in 1933 when Fulgencio Batista led the coup referred to as the Revolt of the Sergeants until January of 1959, Batista had between a thousand and twenty thousand Cubans assassinated (depends on source of data—there is no exact number available), took millions of dollars in kickbacks from American businesses and mafia families, and turned a democratic Cuba in 1933 into a dictatorship designed only to enrich himself and his friends. Notwithstanding Batista's atrocities and criminal behavior, the American giant did nothing, and its government supported the despot with money, military equipment, and logistical support.[15]

Then a senator, John Kennedy, said, "When Batista abandoned Cuba, United States companies owned about 40 percent of the Cuban sugar lands—almost all the cattle ranches—90 percent of the mines and mineral concession—80 percent of the utilities—practically all the oil industry—and supplied two-thirds of Cuba's imports."[16]

Senator Kennedy went on to describe the revolution using realistic descriptions:

---

15 Lillian Guerra, Greg Grandin, and Gilbert Joseph, eds., *Beyond Paradox. A Century of Revolution*, American Encounters/Global Interactions, Durham, NC: Duke University Press, 2010.

16 Senator John F. Kennedy, Remarks at Democratic Dinner, Cincinnati, Ohio, October 6, 1960; John F. Kennedy Presidential Library.

But Castro is not just another Latin American dictator—a petty tyrant bent merely on personal power and gain. His ambitions extend far beyond his own shores. He has transformed the island of Cuba into a hostile and militant Communist satellite—a base from which to carry Communist infiltration and subversion throughout the Americas. With guidance, support, and arms from Moscow and Peiping, he has made anti-Americanism a sign of loyalty and anti-communism a punishable crime—confiscated over a billion dollars' worth of American property—threatened the existence of our naval base at Guantanamo—and rattled red rockets at the United States, which can hardly close its eyes to a potential enemy missile or submarine base only 90 miles from our shores.[17]

Even before Kennedy was president and had access to all available intelligence, he noted that China and Russia worked with Castro to overthrow Batista. I recall clearly the federal government's position that Castro was good for Cuba, but as Kennedy, in the same speech noted, Castro had betrayed the ideals of the Cuban revolution and the hopes of the Cuban people.

The Russians, or at least its leader, Khrushchev, had logical reasons to use Cuba and Castro as pawns in his plans. For example, the United States had more than a hundred missiles deployed in Italy and Turkey in 1961 available to strike anywhere in the Soviet Union. Khrushchev also planned on taking over West Berlin (administered by the United States, Great Britain, and France) and adding its people to Soviet domination. He also was convinced the United States was going to invade Cuba to restore democracy and capitalism. In placing missiles in Cuba, he assumed President Kennedy was inexperienced and would only complain but not take any action to force removal of the missiles once in place. Khrushchev was wrong. President Kennedy woke the sleeping giant, and American ships and planes surrounded the Cuban island.

The missiles and their supporting structures were built, and the United States forced their removal. This lesson is directly relevant to the South China

---

17 Ibid.

Sea. China and Russia both assumed the American giant would not awaken, and the US leadership would not challenge Soviet or Chinese expansion because of fear of confrontation. Russia lost because Kennedy did use the US military to back up demands for the removal of the threat.

China is winning possession of the South China Sea because, since the end of the Vietnam War, the United States has not seriously challenged the communist/Soviet plans of world domination with force; no matter how long it takes, China will win.

GUATEMALA

I am most familiar with the efforts of Cuba and Russia to change Guatemala's political landscape in the 1950s. Jacobo Arbenz was greatly influenced by his wife; she was a socialist and converted her husband to this political philosophy. One of Arbenz's policies that ran afoul of the landholders was his law of agrarian reform. In essence the law took uncultivated land from large corporations (rich) and gave it to the poor.

In 1954 he left office without a fight when the United States supported a Guatemalan army officer who mounted an attack on the government—his name was Carlos Castillo Armas. Yes, he was a puppet of the United States, and he was intent on developing a democratic capitalistic-style government with the help of the Americans. Unfortunately, the communists had him assassinated by his bodyguard while sitting down to dinner with his family in the presidential home. To this day it is uncertain whether Romeo Vasquez, the assassin, was paid or had personal motives for his act.

I was in Tiquisate, headquarters for the United Fruit Company, on July 26, 1957, when the assassination took place. I was sixteen at the time, but I still remember for years not one word was published about the motive behind the act. Nonetheless, the damage was done, and President Armas was followed by several authoritarian leaders who bordered on being dictator-type presidents, resulting in the thirty-six-year civil war starting three years later in 1960.

Thirty-six years of civil war followed with the communist/socialist forces trying to eliminate any Guatemalan trying to live free. The brunt of the killings and atrocities were against the Mayans. Guatemala is slowly recovering from the communist/socialist attempt to take over the government and seems to be doing well. A good source of the details of the attempts, successes, and failures in the history of this Central American country may be found in an excellent research document written by Diane K. Stanley, a retired US Foreign Service officer with roots in Guatemala.[18]

As a result of Russia's interference with Guatemalan politics, the people suffered thirty-six years of war and conflict between successive dictatorial fascist-style governments tending toward communist/socialist policies against indigenous civilian guerillas united as the Guatemalan National Revolutionary Unity. URNG (Spanish abbreviation) became a political party after the 1996 peace accords were signed. The URNG is still a socialist left-wing party. The government, as described, was never clearly defined with a particular political leaning but vacillated among dictatorial, fascist, communist, and socialist leaders. The government that was overthrown under the US-backed Carlos Castillo Armas was working its way toward capitalism and democracy for the Guatemalan people.

Guatemala is lucky; slowly it is overcoming the continued criminal activities and lawlessness that have reigned since the peace was initiated in 1996, but it still has a long way to go. What was the catalyst that plunged Guatemala into almost half a century of war and lawlessness? Had the Russians not interfered with Guatemalan politics by convincing Mrs. Jacobo Arbenz to embrace the Marxist/Leninist concepts of revolution, President Arbenz would not have started Guatemala on the road to war.

VIETNAM

The Soviet Union and China, believing the Marx/Engel manifesto where class struggle and revolution would have communism eradicating capitalism, continued to help countries follow this path. Vietnam was next, having suffered constant struggles to become free of French and Japanese

---

18   Diane K. Stanley, *For the Record: The United Fruit Company's Sixty-Six Years in Guatemala*, Editorial, Antigua, S. A., Guatemala City, Guatemala, 1994.

domination and being divided at the conclusion of World War II into North and South Vietnam, with Russia persuasively convincing Ho Chi Minh to sign the Geneva Accords allowing the partition. The Russian argument was that division would allow time for Ho Chi Minh to consolidate power, undertake economic reform, and improve its military capability. Ho Chi Minh signed the accords, but South Vietnam and the United States did not.

The more relevant terms of the accords were these:

- Vietnam was to become an independent nation, formally ending seventy-five years of French colonialism. Cambodia and Laos were also given their independence.
- Vietnam would be temporarily divided for a period of two years. The border was defined as the line of latitude seventeen degrees north of the equator (the 17th parallel). The accords prescribed the border purely as a means to "settle military questions with a view to ending hostilities...the military demarcation line is provisional and should not in any way be interpreted as constituting a political or territorial boundary."
- Nationwide elections, conducted under international supervision, were scheduled for July 1956. The election result was to determine Vietnam's future political system and government.
- During the two-year transitional period, military personnel were to return to their place of origin: Viet Minh soldiers and guerrillas to North Vietnam, French and pro-French troops to South Vietnam. Vietnamese civilians could relocate to either North or South Vietnam.
- During the transition period, both North and South Vietnam agreed not to enter into any foreign military alliances or authorize the construction of foreign military bases.

Vietnam's transition from being at the mercy of its French masters to its current position in the communist/socialist nations of the world may be used as an example of how a population's behavior is changed from merely wanting to be free and enjoying the rights of all humans to a subjugated mass with no rights. The following list details the struggle of the Vietnamese to be free:

1887–1941	fighting against the French
1941–1945	fighting against the Japanese
1946–1954	fighting against the French
1963–1973	fighting with the United States and other members of the South East Asia Treaty Organization (SEATO) against North Vietnam, Russia, and China
1973–1975	fighting against North Vietnam, aided by China and Russia and ending in the loss of all freedoms

The Geneva Accords were a rushed attempt to help Vietnam heal its wounds and allow the Vietnamese a chance to vote on what type of government they wanted. Elections were to have taken place in 1956. When the United States recommended the United Nations supervise the elections, the Soviet Union used its veto power to quash a potentially fair vote for the Vietnamese people. Since the Soviet Union and Chinese leaders pushed Ho Chi Minh to sign the accords, one must ask, why would an honest attempt to have the UN supervise the elections be opposed by North Vietnam's backers?

The answer is found by understanding the basic premise put forth by Marx and Engels: communism would displace capitalism as a result of eliminating classes of humans in society so every member could produce based on his or her ability, and all would consume based on their needs. Governments would no longer be necessary in such a classless society. As discussed before, Marx and Engels did not accept humans being born with knowledge of their eventual death and an innate desire to live free to enjoy whatever they could create during their life-span. And their ideas ran contrary to the cherished words of the Declaration of Independence that claim for all men, "unalienable Rights that among these are Life, Liberty and the pursuit of Happiness."

The question then becomes how do states control the natural tendency of humans to want life, liberty, and a chance to pursue happiness. Two possibilities have evolved since the mid-1920s. The first is the development of a strong single-party government that has the power to physically remove humans that do not agree to accept the communist/socialist agenda; the second is forced education of the masses starting from birth and continuing until death. Hillary Clinton's mentor and hero, Saul Alinsky, recognized this and proposed a rule for fomenting revolution requiring a government to control the education system in order to properly indoctrinate the young to accept subjugation to a socialist form of rule and economics.

North Vietnam can be used as an example of the first technique. During the period set aside for Vietnam to decide its own future (1953–1956), North Vietnam used the following tactics to convince its population that communism/socialism was preferable to capitalism:

* Agrarian reform was instituted, including "rent reduction" and "land reform." Land was forcibly taken from large landowners and rich peasants and distributed to poor and middle-class peasants as preferential treatment was given to those supporting the Communist Party.[19]

* Mass slaughters of landlords; middle- and upper-class individuals, intellectuals, anticommunists, affiliates with the French colonial government, and dissidents were persecuted, imprisoned, or killed.[20]

* Ho Chi Minh's government had, at a minimum, 14,000 humans executed during the early "rent reduction" campaign.[21]

* Estimates based on the approximate 150,000 houses and huts that were taken by Ho Chi Minh's government and redistributed put land-reform executions between 120,000 and 200,000.[22]

---

19   Qiang Ahai, *China and the Vietnam Wars, 1950–1975*, The University of North Carolina Press, 2000.

20   Anita Lauve Nutt, *On the Question of Communist Reprisals in Vietnam*, Rand, 1970.

21   Alec Holcombe, Politburo's Directive Issued on May 4, 1953, on Some Special Issues regarding Mass Mobilization, *Journal of Vietnamese Studies*, Vol. 5, No. 2 (Summer 2010), 243–47, quoting a translated Politburo directive from May 4, 1953. This directive was published in *Complete Collection of Party Documents* (Van Kien Dang Toan Tap), a fifty-four-volume work authorized by the Vietnamese Communist Party.

22   Lam Thanh Liem, *Ho Chi Minh's Land Reform: Mistake or Crime? Retrieved from http://www. paulbogdanor.com/left/vietnam/landreform.html on May 7, 2016.*

- Official records suggest that 172,008 "landlords" were executed during the "land reform"—approximately 123,266 (71.66 percent) were later found to not be "landlords." This "class" of humans was either shot, beheaded, beaten to death, or crushed to death by rocks. The full death toll from Ho Chi Minh's attempt to remove an entire class of humans was much greater because the government isolated the families of the "landlords," and a vast majority starved to death.[23, 24]
- Hoang Van Chi, a former Viet Minh official, believed that as many as 500,000 people may have died as a result of the policies of the Ho Chi Minh government.[25]
- Humans who were members of groups that opposed the Ho Chi Minh government were imprisoned in hard labor camps and abused, beaten, subjected to intensive hard labor, and died of exhaustion, starvation, illness, or assaults by prison guards. Private property ownership, large businesses, and entrepreneurship were criminalized.[26]

These listed atrocities followed the examples set by the Soviet Union and China in every country where the two communist giants attempted and most often succeeded in establishing totalitarian governments using communism/socialism as their standard. The prime example is Mao Tse-tung's Hundred Flowers Campaign, started in 1956 to "entice the snakes out of their caves." The snakes, of course, were any humans who disagreed with the Communist Party of China, who, when identified, were promptly executed or imprisoned in labor camps.

While all the previously mentioned atrocities were taking place, the American giant slept, and the country did not have a clue about what was going on with Russian and Chinese support of the Vietnamese communists (Viet Minh) and their goals for adding Vietnam to the growing roster of

---

23 *The History of the Vietnamese Economy*, Vol. 2, edited by Dang Phong of the Institute of Economy, Vietnamese Institute of Social Sciences, 2005.

24 Paul Bogdanor, "The Blood-Red Hands of Ho Chi Minh," *Readers Digest*, November 1968.

25 Hoang Van Chi, *From Colonialism to Communism: A Case Study of North Vietnam*, New York: Congress of Cultural Freedom, 1962.

26 Steven Rosefielde, *Red Holocaust*, New York: Routledge, 2009.

communist/socialist countries. Prior to and after the duration of the Southeast Asia Treaty Organization (SEATO)—countries attempting to stop the expansion and enslavement of the Vietnamese people—Russia and China worked together for world domination.

During the Vietnam War between the early 1960s and the mid-1970s, Russia and China were at odds with each other on how to proceed with world domination. Therefore, the support of the Vietnamese communists and Ho Chi Minh was bifurcated between the two.

Before analyzing how Russia and China backed Vietnam's subjugation by communism/socialism, it is important to understand the Vietnamese communist leader, Ho Chi Minh. Even though I was a military officer fighting in Vietnam (1966–1967) and did many briefings on the origin of the conflict, I was never aware of Ho Chi Minh's communist/socialist roots. I proffer that very few citizens in the world knew of his background and ultimate goals.

Based on his specific goal of unifying Vietnam as an independent communist/socialist country, Ho realized this goal could not be achieved without the help of Russia and China. To better understand Ho's mind-set, his education and history prior to the 1960s must be understood. The following information was obtained from multiple sources, and as previously noted this is not a research paper, so the numerous references consulted are not listed. On the other hand, the information provided is considered accurate by this writer.

Ho Chi Minh used many names prior to settling on "Ho Chi Minh" in 1940. (Translated from Sino-Vietnamese, Ho's chosen name reads, "He who has been enlightened and is a bright spirit.") Ho, as Nguyen Sinh Cung, was first noticed when he became interested in Marxism after the failure of Vietnam to gain its independence from France at the end of World War I. In a letter dated June 18, 1919, Ho (as Nguyen Ai Quoc) pleaded with the American secretary of state, Robert Lansing, at the Paris Peace Conference, to help the Annamite (Vietnamese people) gain their independence from France. His letter was ignored without a response from the American delegation. Naturally Ho was possibly depressed for having failed to get the attention of the peace delegation.

He remained in Paris, and based on a memorandum Ho wrote in 1960 describing his "path" leading to Leninism, worked as a retoucher of photographs and a painter of "Chinese antiquities" (made in France!). The reason he gave for joining the French Socialist Party was that its members showed sympathy toward him and the struggle of the Annamite people against France.

Ho raised a question concerning which dogma of the branches of the Socialist Party would be best for a colonized country such as French Indochina. He was given a copy of Lenin's "Thesis on the National and Colonial Questions." From his readings and further learnings from attending Socialist Party meetings, Ho developed his position of "nationalism" and that only socialism and communism could liberate the oppressed nations and the working people throughout the world from slavery. Leninism was Ho's compass for the Vietnamese revolutionaries and people; it was also the radiant sun illuminating the path to final victory, to socialism and communism.[27]

At the end of World War II, the Western allies, including the American giant, failed to listen to the pleas of the Vietnamese by returning French Indochina to the French. During 1945 and 1946 Ho pleaded with the United States for recognition of the independence of the Democratic Republic of Vietnam (DRV) or, in the alternative, have the DRV become a trustee under the United Nations. All his efforts were ignored so as to support the French control of its colonies in Indochina.

The United States actually supported the French financially from 1946 until their withdrawal after the fall of Dien Bien Phu on May 7, 1954. The historical perspective of the US support of the French seems to be linked directly with President Eisenhower's explanation of the fear that if Vietnam came under socialist/communist control, the rest of Southeast Asia would fall like "dominoes" under the efforts of China and Russia to dominate the world. It now appears that Eisenhower was correct.

The battle for Dien Bien Phu was continuing when the delegates were convening in April 1954 for the Geneva Conference among Vietnam, China, and the United States to discuss the future of Indochina. The Vietnamese

---

27 Nguyen Ai Quoc (Ho Chi Minh), *The Path Which Led Me to Leninism*, 1960, accessed at http://vietnamwar.lib.umb.edu/origins/docs/Lansing.html.

communists achieved victory the day before the conference convened on May 8. The first of two agreements was approved by all parties—France and the Vietnamese communists (Viet Minh) would cease all hostilities, and Vietnam would be temporarily divided along the 17th parallel. French forces would remain in the South, and Ho Chi Minh's forces would control the North.

The second agreement was not approved by the United States for very good reason: because it contained a provision that neither the Vietnamese communists nor the South would join an alliance with an outside party. The United Nations had just concluded hostilities in Korea on or about July 27, 1953. As noted before, the Korean communists allied with Russia and China to defeat the United Nations by holding them to a draw along the original division parallel. The United States and the state of Vietnam (South) feared, and perhaps rightfully so, that China and Russia would come to the aid of Ho Chi Minh to ensure the continued expansion of communism/socialism, no matter what agreements had been signed.

In July, after the Geneva Convention convened, Zhou En-lai met with Ho Chi Minh to discuss how to keep the United States from siding with the South and how long it would take General Vo Nguyen Giap (General Giap) to defeat the French, assuming they were reinforced, and capture all of Indochina. General Giap proffered it would take three to five years. With the United States intervening on behalf of South Vietnam, it actually took from 1954 until 1973 (nineteen years) for the communist/socialists to take control of the majority of Indochina.

American citizens were not aware that the United States, as leader of the Southeast Asia Treaty Organization, was really engaged in battle with General Giap's Viet Minh (Viet Cong), who were being supplied and advised by Russia and China. I will leave the discussion of the poor choice the United States made in initially backing then-President Ngo Dinh Diem in South Vietnam for another book and focus on the Russian/Chinese backing of the Viet Nam Cong San (Viet Cong) and Viet Minh (Vietnam's communist organizations).

Ho Chi Minh was always a "nationalist" who was concerned only with consolidating Vietnam and its people into one country. At first, as noted earlier, he tried multiple times to gain favor with the United States and get help with his anticolonization efforts to gain freedom from France. By the early 1950s, he was convinced of the benefits, as he saw them, of Lenin's ideas and set a goal for Vietnam to become an independent communist/socialist country, but never did he want to be subservient to the Russian or Chinese communist/socialist parties. And at the same time he realized his Viet Minh could not separate from France and establish his ideal communist/socialist country with their help. Russia and China also believed, as they still do today, it would serve their world domination goals to ensure all of Asia was communist/socialist.

At the end of World War II, Russia gave only marginal support to the communist/socialist movement in Vietnam. Stalin wanted to maintain a postwar alliance with the West and tried to do so by playing down his support of the Viet Minh between the end of World War I and 1948. The political climate for Moscow changed drastically when Mao, with Russia's help as noted before, was successful in pushing Chiang Kai-shek off the mainland of China.

In 1950 Moscow changed its position and recognized Ho Chi Minh and the Viet Minh as the "official" rulers of Vietnam. The change of position was also based on the American, French, and British positions that Russia did not honor its agreement at the end of World War II by refusing to remove its troops from Czechoslovakia, Rumania, Hungary, and Poland and by using the KGB to stifle any opposition in these countries against communism and socialism.

To emphasize his desire to force as many people and countries under the communist/socialist umbrella, Stalin blockaded Berlin in an attempt to force West Berliners under his control. Perhaps Stalin was reacting to the formation of Bizonia, in which the United States and Britain combined the areas of Berlin they controlled in 1947. France joined her area to Bizonia, forming Trizonia. Stalin eventually had to recognize the new Germany (Trizonia) but did gain the temporary right to keep East Germany under communist/socialist rule.

Meanwhile, the Chinese during the immediate post–World War II period were working with the Viet Minh. Chinese communist forces often retreated into North Vietnam to rest and prepare for future offensives. In return for sanctuary, China provided the Viet Minh with weapons, munitions, and training. China continued providing significant amounts of military aid to the Viet Minh while they were also supplying North Korea (1950–1953). These supplies were transported into French Indochina down the jungle routes, which were the forerunners of the Ho Chi Minh trail.

The support of China was best characterized as unconditional support and a blank check for supplies and equipment. The Chinese promise came to an end sometime between 1965 and 1968 when tensions escalated between Mao and various Russian leaders. Before the end of its support, China had provided North Vietnam with equipment (trucks, tanks, and artillery) and construction projects in the form of several thousand engineering troops to assist in building and repairing railways, runways, roads, and military defense positions. Over 320,000 Chinese troops were stationed in North Vietnam during the period of the war with the peak of 170,000 in 1967.

The Soviets did not reestablish support until Aleksei Kosygin notified the world of Soviet recognition of the National Liberation Front (NLF or Viet Cong) and then visited North Vietnam in February 1965. Kosygin signed a treaty with North Vietnam promising financial aid, military equipment, and advisors. This they did—during Operation Rolling Thunder sophisticated Soviet-supplied air-defense systems were able to down 922 US aircraft.

Notwithstanding the massive support by Russia and China afforded to the North Vietnamese, Operation Rolling Thunder was controlled from Washington—micromanaged would be a better description. The military wanted to close Haiphong and all ports being used by the Soviets to supply North Vietnam, but US forces were instructed to observe restrictions—for example, airstrikes were forbidden within sixty kilometers of Hanoi and within nineteen kilometers of the port of Haiphong, and a thirty-mile no-bombing zone extended along the length of the Chinese frontier. The political reason voiced by Washington was that the United States did not want to go to war with Russia or China or both. The eventual war with these countries was put off until another day.

INDIA

India and China have had an up-and-down geopolitical relationship since the beginning of time. China's 1962 October invasion of the sovereign territory of India can be used to support a modern-day understanding of what to expect China's behavior would be in the South China Sea dispute. The current version of history has Premier Zhou En-lai being in favor of solving the border issue with India through negotiations.[28] Nehru refused to negotiate in compliance with the political position of his party, and the invasion was necessary to bring India to the negotiating table.[29] Ananth Krishnan, and expert in India – China relations, also mentions the 1959 Tibet uprising, and India granting the Dalai Lama exile in India was probably another reason for the invasion. If one takes into account India's claim based on the Johnson Line of 1865 and China's claim line of 1960, which it reached militarily in 1962, it appears China added approximately 36,000 square miles to its territory—a land mass larger than Maryland and smaller than West Virginia.

The area acquired by China's aggression is of no practical geopolitical value; its average elevation exceeds 16,000 feet, which is higher than Pikes Peak in Colorado and Mount Whitney, the highest peaks in the contiguous forty-eight states. Peaks in the area taken by China almost reach the height of Mount McKinley (Denali) at 20,320 feet. Most humans (75 percent) need supplemental oxygen above 10,000 feet, and those living at 16,000 feet and above need to acclimatize to avoid Acute Mountain Sickness (AMS).[30] So what prompted the Chinese to kill 1,383 Indian military personnel and capture 3,968?[31]

Since no records could be found to document the actual intent of Mao's government, perhaps linking all the encroachments made by the Chinese into other countries together will help. The common thread seems to be based in

---

28 Ananth Krishnan, "1962 War Detrimental to Both India and China," *The Hindu*, December 13, 2012, accessed at: http://www.thehindu.com/news/international/1962-war-detrimental-to-both-india-and-china/article4195469.ece?css=print.

29 Ibid.

30 Rick Curtis, *Outdoor Action Guide to High Altitude: Acclimatization and Illnesses*, accessed at www.princeton.edu/~oa/safety/altitude.html.

31 "War File: Sino-Indian War," accessed at www.historyguy.com/warfiles/sino-indian_war_warfile.htm#.VMFbyS4v2ac.

the Marx/Lenin (Stalin/Mao) desires to convert all countries of the world to the communist/socialist model. And lurking in the background perhaps was Mao's intent to distract the citizens of China from realizing that being free to live as they wish would lead to better economics and living conditions. By linking together China's acts of aggressive behavior and ignoring the rhetoric of the Chinese leaders, the ultimate goal of world domination becomes evident.

Hans Morgenthau stated this concept best by noting that states will comply with international law only when to do so is to their benefit for consolidating or amassing power.[32] If Morgenthau is correct, China will continue to do what is necessary to maximize the power of the CCP. It will possibly choose two of the three methods outlined by Morgenthau for maximizing power: seek to preserve the status quo and seek to demonstrate power and gain prestige. China provides an excellent example of Morgenthau's ideas.

Lt. Michael Studeman, USN, in the spring of 1998 published a paper for the Army War College containing an excellent argument. Essentially Studeman argues that the CCP realized in the late 1970s that revolution was becoming unreliable as a source of social cohesion in China and that an alternative was needed for the CCP to ensure its survival and maximize its power. As a result of this realization, the party turned to nationalism, its ability to protect and defend China's sovereignty, and expand its sovereignty over its neighbors, including the entire South China Sea. By so doing, the CCP committed itself to holding Taiwan, Hong Kong, Tibet, Xinjiang, *Macao, the Paracels*, and the Spratlys (italicized entries are my additions to Lt. Studeman's list).[33]

Other experts feel international law is voluntary. Professor Henkin states, "Almost all nations observe almost all principles of international law and almost all of their obligations almost all of the time"..."no government will

---

32 Hans J. Morgenthau, *Politics among Nations: The Struggle for Power and Peace*, 1988, 86–100.

33 Michael Studeman, "Calculating China's Advances in the South China Sea: Identifying the Triggers of 'Expansionism,'" *Naval War College Review* 51, no. 2 (Spring 1998), accessed at http://www.globalsecurity.org/military/library/report/1998/art5-sp8.htm (last modified Spring 1998).

observe international law in the crunch, when it really hurts."[34] Friedmann continues by saying, "International law is a simple matter of 'realism' versus 'wishful thinking.'"[35]

These "out of context" quotes illustrate that there is no one body of agreement on whether international law, as embodied in UNCLOS III, is really accepted law notwithstanding the "treaty" nature of the convention. Starting with the appeasement of China in ousting Taiwan and giving China a permanent seat at the United Nations, American leaders continue to believe that China will eventually become an international-law-abiding state of the world; based upon China's history since 1927, our leaders appear to be ignoring the reality of China's and Russia's goal of world domination.

SOUTH CHINA SEA

This section will be devoted only to the chronology of China's aggression in the South China Sea as related to the littoral nations on this sea. China, as a recognized country, seems to have been established about 222 BCE when Qin Shi-huang conquered six other kingdoms and established the first unified state. Between the establishment this country and the early 1970s, the Chinese never addressed the issue of sovereignty over the formations in the South China Sea. China's 1974 attack on Vietnam's Paracel Islands is discussed elsewhere in this book.

These events started China's aggression to gain possession of all the formations in the sea. China has developed disputes with Brunei, Malaysia, the Philippines, Vietnam, and Indonesia. China has also become aggressive with Japan concerning the Senkaku/Diaoyu Island chain.

The timing of China's aggression against the Vietnamese formations (such as the islets and rocks) was well timed. The US involvement in Vietnam was coming to an end, and the Chinese were well aware of the opposition to the war by some citizens of the United States. The mainstream media published

---

34 Damroasch, Henkin, Pugh, Schachter, Smit, *International Law*, 1393, West Group, American Casebook Series, 2001.

35 Ibid.

sufficient negative information supporting the concept that US politicians were being influenced by the antiwar feelings of a percentage of citizens. President Nixon also visited China in 1972 to establish diplomatic relations, through which the United States abandoned its support of Taiwan. He also ended the US military draft and initiated détente and the Anti-Ballistic Missile Treaty with the Soviet Union. Then there was Watergate and Nixon's resignation in August 1974.

China was still recovering from Mao's attempt to institute a Great Leap Forward, which was the direct cause of approximately 34 million people (5 percent of China's population) starving to death. This fiasco was followed by Mao's Cultural Revolution, with its severe radical phase coming to an end in 1971 with the failed coup d'état and the death of its leader, Lin Biao.

The United States continued to court China's favor with President Ford's meeting with Deng Xiao-ping in 1975. It is important to remember that the US intelligence services and therefore our presidents must have been aware that we lost South Vietnam to communism/socialism because Russia and China provided the necessary financial and military arms support to the North. Therefore, one must question the advisability of courting the favor of the Chinese communist/socialist regime.

Chinese leadership must have read the tea leaves correctly because the United States in 1974 failed to support Vietnam when the Chinese attacked their island in the South Pacific. Starting with this first aggressive action by China and probably confident the United States would never intervene and protect its commitments to the littoral nations and the South China Sea for forty years, China has continued aggressively dominating the sea, and the United States has done nothing. Sending one ship on a transit bordering the twelve-nautical-mile faux-territorial sea limit surrounding an artificial structure built on a reef does nothing more than provide recognition of China's claim to the ocean formation. It would be impressive if the Obama administration ordered a US Navy warship to peacefully transit the faux-territorial sea in accordance with the provisions of UNCLOS III and even have a landing party visit the formation. By so doing the transit and landing would provide recognition of the sovereignty another nation—say the Philippines.

PANAMA

The Chinese government, as of the passing of "Law 5" on January 16, 1997, controls the Panama Canal and has the power to shut it down whenever it wishes. The pilot-boat crews working the canal are manned by troops from the People's Liberation Army Navy of China (approximately 25 percent of the total crew). President Bill Clinton and his administration allowed this to happen without one word of protest. Law 5 came about because the Panamanian government was bribed with bucketloads of cash given to them under the table by the Chinese. During the first round of bids for leasing defensive positions at both ends of the canal, the Chinese corporation, Hutchison Whampoa, came in fourth behind the US firm Bechtel, Panamanian-American Company M.I.T., and the highest bidder, Japan's Kawasaki/I.T.S.

In his book *The China Threat*, Bill Gertz outlined how China's conglomerate, Hutchison Whampoa, was spreading large sums of cash in Panama with a goal of being awarded the leases of canal property at both Balboa and Cristobal. The subterfuge of the People's Republic of China to gain control of the Panama Canal runs deep, and it will take complete dedication of the US armed forces to dislodge them from the Panama Canal. The terms of the leases between the Republic of Panama and Hutchison Whampoa, Ltd., a puppet of the Chinese government, in their final forms did not resemble the original offer on which all initial bids were made. The United States Customs Service reporting on these issues stated Hutchison Whampoa won the port contracts through an unfair and corrupt contractual bidding process. For a complete description of the deceit and illegal activities of the People's Republic of China in obtaining control of the Panama Canal, one only needs to read Gertz's book, particularly the subchapter "A Strategic Coup." China's act of acquiring control of the Panama Canal gives it the power to close the canal when it so desires.

CAMBODIA, VIETNAM, CHINA

Ambassador John Gunther Dean, following orders from President Gerald Ford and Secretary of State Henry Kissinger, led the US retreat from Cambodia on

April 12, 1975. This failure in Cambodia followed several years of the United States and the Republic of South Vietnam invading the country in a futile attempt to dislodge the North Vietnamese communist troops from their hold on eastern Cambodia.

Five days after the departure of the United States, on April 17, 1975, the Communist Party of Kampuchea (CPK) took control of Cambodia and ruled the country until January 1979. This era became known as the rule of Pol Pot. During his rule, an estimated two million dissenting Cambodians where murdered by his regime. The United States did nothing. China also rushed into Cambodia to support Pol Pot's regime in the name of communism and world domination. China was anxious to fill the vacuum left by the departure of the United States when it abandoned Cambodia. China provided the Government of Democratic Kampuchea (Cambodia) a complete arsenal of weapons augmented by approximately fifteen thousand advisors to support the Khmer Rouge regime—the United States and the United Nations again did nothing.

In 1975 and 1977, there were many clashes between the Pol Pot government and the Socialist Republic of Vietnam (former North Vietnam). The currently accepted reason for the Cambodians' constantly harassing the Vietnamese was a fear that Vietnam wanted to dominate the entire Indonesian peninsula. Vietnam, depending on an agreement with the Soviet Union, attacked Cambodia in December 1978, completing its advance when it captured Phnom Penh on January 7, 1979. Between 1979 and 1989, the Vietnamese ruled Cambodia and left peacefully in September.[36]

As previously discussed, President Nixon visited China in February of 1972 and announced to the world that his visit changed the world. Apparently China did not agree with President Nixon's optimism because it aligned itself with the Khmer Rouge and their communist doctrine of world domination. Also China was on the outs with the Soviet Union, and the Soviets signed a mutual defense treaty with Vietnam on April 17, 1975, bolstering the Soviet effort to contain China's version of communism as previously discussed herein.

---

36 I use the name "Cambodia" rather than shifting back and forth with "Kampuchea," which is Cambodia in the Khmer language.

It is important to tie all of China's foreign policy decisions during this time frame together as a good indicator of China's continued goal of world domination. Their invasion of the Paracel Islands on January 19, 1974, killing many Vietnamese and taking possession of the island chain by force was an excellent example of attacking when the United States attention was diverted. The world did nothing. China is still in possession of the Paracel Island group, and because the United States and the world did nothing to stop this expansion of China's control of the South China Sea, the act most likely provided China's leadership with confidence that they could take over the entire South China Sea and no nation would stop them.

China, notwithstanding its political posture presented to President Nixon's party and Secretary of State Kissinger, warned Vietnam not to interfere with the Pol Pot regime. Vietnam continued its assault on Phnom Penh and was occupying the city when China invaded Vietnam on February 17, 1979, and retreated on March 16, claiming victory. On the other hand, their invasion of Vietnam did not affect the Vietnamese effort in Cambodia, which eventually led to an end of the murderous Pol Pot regime and the restoration of the Cambodian monarchy. The Chinese took a savage beating by the better-trained and battle-hardened Vietnamese using American weapons left in Vietnam after the Southeast Asia Treaty Organization failed to stop communist expansion into South Vietnam.

The beating of the People's Liberation Army by the Vietnamese highlights a reality not considered by the mainstream media in the United States. Chinese forces are not battle tested—this short-lived invasion of Vietnam was the PLA's last engagement. This is of course if one does not count the deployment of the PLA against its own citizens in 1984 in Tiananmen Square.

There is one demographic in China's favor: as a result of its one-child policy, China now has approximately 33 million more males than females. These men provide China's Communist Party with what could be referred to as a disposable army. They become disposable because they do not have wives and children to care whether or not they are killed in battle. The United States has the opposite problem: in 2000 there were approximately 3 million more women than men.

The Future for China on the World Stage

China will continue to ignore international law until it is in its best interest to change its behavior on the world stage. Since the 1970s major world leaders have focused their attention on other parts of the earth and have been ignoring China's continued march toward world domination. As with drug addicts, recalcitrant children, and rogue nations, intervention must be strong, decisive, and relentless until China determines its best interest is to ameliorate its aberrant behavior and take its rightful place among other nations, giving up its goal of dominating the world's population. Now is the time to draw a line in the sand and for the United States and its allies to stop China from adding the South China Sea to its empire.

CHAPTER 2

Analysis of China's Deception and Summary of Historical Arguments

---

FOLKLORE AND HEARSAY SAY THAT one must observe the behavior of an individual carefully and not listen to what the person says in order to predict his or her future behavior or value system. Does it not follow that "observed behavior" is also true of states such as the People's Republic of China?

Stuart Harris of Pacifica Review states this same concept more elegantly: "Relying on official statements is never a totally reliable process for analyzing any country but especially in China's case. The lack of transparency of the Chinese system leaves unclear what are the motivations of the Chinese leadership."[37]

On May 15, 1996, the People's Republic of China filed its "Declaration of the Government of the People's Republic of China on the baselines of the territorial sea, 15 May 1996."[38] The PRC was allegedly complying with its agreement to file the specific coordinates (latitude and longitude) as required by Article 16 of the United Nations Law of the Sea on which the state intended to establish its maritime baseline.[39]

The Paracel Islands' baseline shown in the following map was prepared using the geographic positions filed by the Chinese government.

---

37   Stuart Harris, "China and the Pursuit of State Interests in a Globalizing World," *13 Pacifica Rev.* (2001): 15–16.
38   "Deposit of charts/lists of coordinates under the convention," accessed at www.un.org/Depts/los/index.htm.
39   UNCLOS III.

Figure 1. Paracel Islands with Baselines

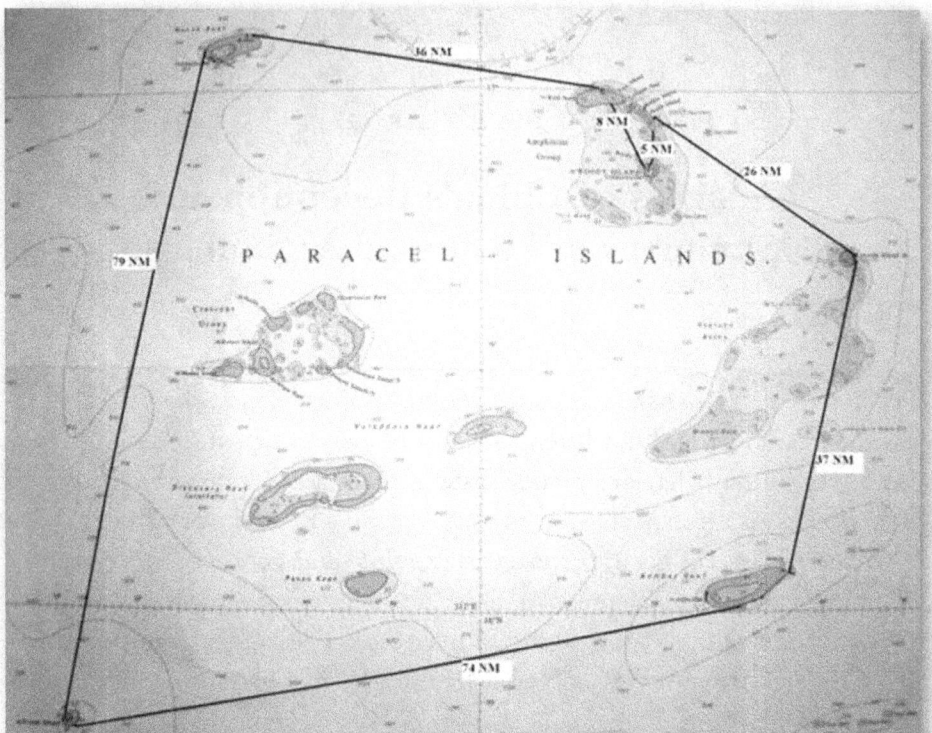

This map represents baselines for determining territorial waters around the Paracel Islands. These baselines do not conform to the guidelines agreed to by the People's Republic of China when it ratified UNCLOS III. Specifically, Part II, Territorial Sea and Contiguous Zone; Section 2. Limits of the Territorial Sea; Article 6, Reefs states: "In the case of islands situated on atolls or of islands having fringing reefs, the baseline for measuring the breadth of the territorial sea is the seaward low-water line of the reef." Woody Island is the only formation that *may* be classified as an island. If none of the formations in the Paracel Islands is considered an island as defined by UNCOLS III, then the area would be considered "high seas" *with sovereignty of the formations disputed by Vietnam.*

For analysis only, assume that the People's Republic of China is able to convince the United Nations (or a tribunal) that Woody Island as required by Article 121(3) is an island and convince Vietnam that Woody Island is the sovereign territory of China. Once these two major hurdles have been cleared, then, and only then, could China file the Article 16 baseline requirements with the United Nations. The PRC ratified UNCLOS III on May 15, 1996, and on June 7 deposited the baseline coordinates for the Paracel Islands. The baseline was 526 kilometers long as plotted on the map shown here.

In essence, the People's Republic of China claimed disputed territory of the high seas merely by depositing the coordinates of the alleged baseline with the United Nations of the disputed area when they ratified the convention.

UNCLOS III, Article 47, Archipelagic baselines, paragraph 2, restricts archipelagic baselines to 100 nautical miles (185.2 kilometers); paragraph 3 provides for a maximum length of 125 nautical miles (231.5 kilometers) for the combined total of all legs of an archipelagic baseline. In addition to this requirement, there is another major requirement based on the ratio of land to water as enclosed within the baselines. Paragraph 1 restricts this water-to-land ratio to between one to one and one to nine.

The previous map, drawn using the latitude and longitude positions submitted by China, far exceeds the maximum ratio provided by UNCLOS III, which was ratified by China. In the revised chart that follows, drawn in an attempt to allow for the fantasy that Vietnam would concede sovereignty to China, Woody Island is an "island," and stretching the definition of "immediate vicinity," the ratio of water to land still exceeds the maximum of 1:9.

Compounding the disregard for the convention signed by the People's Republic of China in regard to filing a baseline, it should also be noted how the convention defines an "archipelagic state." It is defined as a state consisting *wholly* of one or more archipelagoes and may include other islands and archipelagoes. An "archipelago" is defined as a group of islands, including parts of islands, interconnecting waters, and other natural features, which are so closely interrelated that such islands, waters, and other natural features form an intrinsic geographical, economic, and political entity, or which historically have been regarded as such.

China used Part IV ARCHIPELAGIC STATES, Article 47, Archipelagic baselines as the basis for submission when the state is not an archipelagic state. Such is the case of the Paracel Island baselines. The members of the Law of the Sea Convention must not have foreseen countries would claim sovereignty over a group of islands when they were not an archipelagic state even though the United States had done so for the Hawaiian Islands. True, the Hawaiian Islands did not present the problem found in analyzing the Spratly, Paracel, and Scarborough Reef situations. There was no question concerning the ability of the Hawaiian Islands being able to support human populations and economic viability on their own.

By putting all these fraudulent submissions together, it is obvious China has no respect for the convention that its government signed and thereby promised its ratification of the treaty to comply with its terms. These issues were brought to the attention of the United Nations, and no action was taken; the complaints of the United States and the Philippines were completely ignored because China has veto power to block any issue presented to the UN that it does not like. Perhaps the world, including the United States, is afraid of a belligerent China and is therefore using appeasement as the United Kingdom and the United States did with Germany prior to World War II.

It also is unusual for a state to claim territory merely by filing a document with the United Nations when it knows there is a dispute over the territory. Vietnam has been anything but silent on the issue of the Paracels since they were taken from them by force, with the Chinese killing its citizens in the 1974 sea and land battle. The Vietnamese occupation of the Paracels and its administration of the islands gave notice to the world that Vietnam claimed sovereignty of the Paracel Islands.

The People's Republic of China, by filing its baseline coordinates for the Paracels with the United Nations, apparently wants Vietnam to accept its position that the Paracel islets will be used to claim an exclusive economic zone and a continental shelf. No organization, including the UN itself, has questioned this use of islets for baseline determination. And it appears the United Nations does not have a staff person responsible for checking for compliance with the terms of UNLOS III when baseline charts are submitted in accordance with Article 16. Apparently they are received and filed without analysis.

Continuing this line of analysis, we can refer to the charts presented earlier and notice that the distance between Woody Island (islet) and the two islets to the north are five and eight nautical miles respectively. Since China is not an "archipelagic state," only "fringing reefs" can be joined by baselines, and the islets must attach directly to the island or be located in the immediate vicinity. If the PRC was able to convince the United Nations' members that five and eight nautical miles is in the "immediate vicinity," then the baseline would appear as it is indicated in the following map.

Figure 2. "Immediate Vicinity" Distortion—UNCLOS III

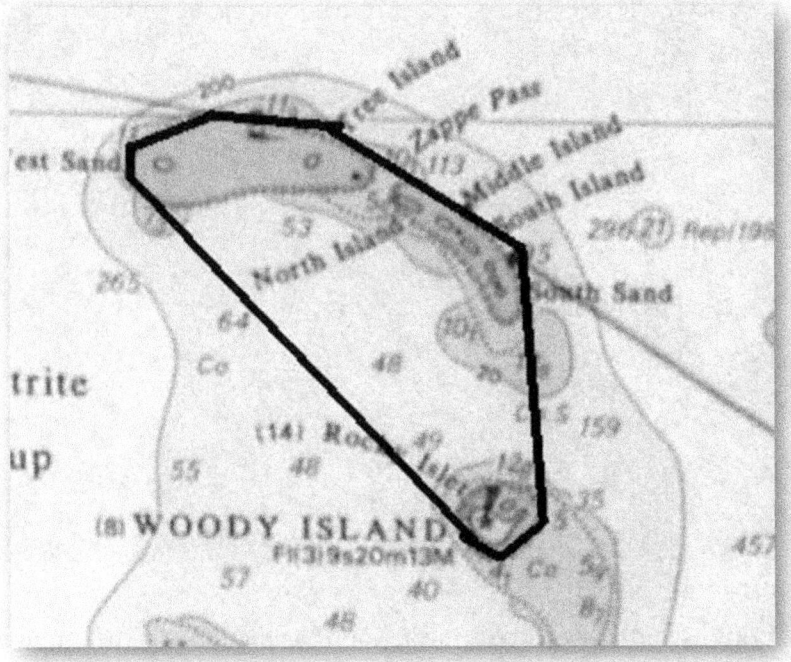

There is no definition of "immediate vicinity" in the *Consolidated Glossary of Technical Terms,* so perhaps a plain English interpretation should be used. In the basic part of the definition, the fringing reef must be "attached directly" to the shore. It follows that "immediate vicinity" would be interpreted as "nearly" attached directly to the shore. Therefore, the correct filing of a baseline for Woody Island would be the outer low-water tide line using the fringing reef attached to an island and not the outlying reefs or islets.

Arriving at this conclusion generates the issue of what to do about the islets that make up the remainder of the Paracels. The best argument a sovereign state would have is that each islet has a territorial sea and contiguous zone of its own with no exclusive economic zone or continental shelf. This argument may be possible once sovereignty is established.

Figure 3. Woody Island—Paracels

Woody Island is the closest formation that may satisfy the requirements of Article 121(1) and 121(3) of UNCLOS III for "island" classification. It still lacks the essentials of water, food, and fuel produced or found on the formation. A close observation of this Digital Globe image from above the island reveals that it does have vegetation, consisting of mangroves and scrubs. China could argue that if mangroves and scrubs can grow on the island with only natural rain irrigation, then the formation qualifies under UNCLOS for island status. On the other hand, would there be sufficient rainfall for human consumption and survival and crop irrigation?

The administrators obviously do not think that natural rainfall is sufficient, and no gardens or hot-houses were observed in the satellite image. The Chinese have gone to great lengths to plant coconut groves and have placed numerous stelae on the island indicating ownership. There are even large office complexes and structures. These were probably developed so the Chinese could argue that they are satisfying the "administrative duties" required to establish and maintain sovereignty over Woody Island. These structures, built after their invasion of the island, should have no effect on any sovereignty decision to settle the dispute between China and Vietnam. China will probably continue to force bilateral negotiations using their wealth and military power to force Vietnam to concede sovereignty. Should this happen the world must not forget China's ultimate goal of claiming Woody Island is an Article 121(3) "island" and should have its own exclusive economic zone.

If none of the formations in the Paracels are islands, then even if China were to be recognized as the sovereign, the largest area of the high seas surrounding the formations that could be claimed would consist of territorial seas and contiguous zones extending twenty-four miles from the baseline. The baseline would be drawn as if the islands were part of the Chinese mainland in view of the fact that China is not an archipelagic state as discussed before. The Paracels would then be located in the exclusive economic zone (EEZ) of Vietnam, and their argument of China's infringement of their rights to control the use of any hydrocarbons found in their EEZ should be upheld by any impartial tribunal.

Islets, such as West Sand and North Island found on the *Paracel Islands with Baselines* are not defined in UNCLOS III. E. D. Brown does an excellent analysis of this issue using the following logic and language contained in UNCLOS III:

1. Article 6 (reefs) only specifies "fringing reefs" as the basis for establishing the baseline for an island situated on an atoll or an island.
2. Article 13 (low-tide elevations) of UNCLOS III defines a low-tide elevation as "a naturally formed area of land which is surrounded by and above water at low-tide but submerged at high tide."
3. Article 121 (regime of islands) defines "islands" as
   a. Naturally formed area of land, surrounded by water, which is above water at high tide.
   b. Rocks that cannot sustain human habitation or economic life of their own shall have no exclusive economic zone or continental shelf.
4. UNCLOS does not define a "rock," but the *Consolidated Glossary* for UNCLOS does define a rock as "a solid mass of limited extent." The *Glossary* also parrots Article 121(3) of UNCLOS: "Rocks which cannot sustain human habitation or economic life of their own shall have no exclusive economic zone or continental shelf." Note that rocks are quasi islands by definition (above water at high tide) but are prevented from supporting exclusive economic zones.
5. Brown concludes that the determination of baselines is not affected by these definitions but only limits "islands" to having EEZs and/or continental shelves.[40]

Building on Brown, consider the absence of definitions for reefs, islets, submerged reefs, fringing reefs, atolls, rocks (as related to formations protruding from the surface of the oceans), banks, and shoals in UNCLOS III; only islands and low-tide elevations are defined with any specificity (rocks).

The People's Republic of China has consistently used the phrase "indisputable sovereignty" when its government leaders refer to the formations in the South China Sea, and they have been doing this since the mid-1970s. The first shot fired in anger over possession of one of the South China Sea's formations in the Paracel Island group invasion was in January 1974. The Chinese

---

40 Brown, E. D. "The International Law of the Sea, Volume I, Introductory Manual", Dartmouth Publishing Company Brookfield, USA, 1994

killed fifty-three South Vietnamese combatants, and they lost eighteen in the process of ousting the Vietnamese from the Paracels. The Chinese were the ultimate winners of the short-lived gun battle. On the other hand, the Democratic Republic of North Vietnam representative was reported to have told the Hungarian Ambassador to Hanoi that there are many documents and data about the islands in question [Paracels] are Vietnamese.

Other North Vietnamese diplomatic sources expressed the opinion that the dispute between China and South Vietnam was temporary and later the problem would affect the whole Vietnamese nation (now the Socialist Republic of Vietnam). This prediction came true, as even today the Socialist Republic of Vietnam continues to claim the Paracels.[41, 42]

The timing of the January 1974 attack by China is critical to understanding how the Chinese leaders take advantage of timing in their foreign-policy strategy. The attack on the Paracels in the South China Sea occurred almost to the day one year after January 27, 1973, the day the Paris Peace Accords were agreed to and placed in effect. The United States was dealing with the aftermath of Watergate, the impeachment of Richard Nixon, and the withdrawal from and loss of Vietnam to the communist regime of the Democratic Republic of North Vietnam.

The Vietnamese continue to protest the taking of the Paracel Islands by force, but the world is not listening. The American sleeping giant continues to ignore the important fact that China violated international law by taking the territory by force. Acquiring land, in this case ocean formations, by force is one of the basic tenets of international civil behavior as codified in international law. The Chinese went to a lot of trouble to oust Taiwan as a member of the United Nations, and the American giant, and its citizens, did nothing while the federal government abandoned Taiwan and the nationalist

---

41 Balázs Szalontai, "Im lặng nhưng không đồng tình," BBC Vietnam, March 24, 2009, accessed at http://www.bbc.co.uk/vietnamese/vietnam/2009/03/090324_paracels_hanoi_reassessment.shtml. The English text of the article ("Silence But No Consent: Hanoi and the Chinese Invasion of the Paracel Islands," 1974) is accessed at https://www.academia.edu/6212210/Silence_But_No_Consent_Hanoi_and_the_Chinese_Invasion_of_the_Paracel_Islands_1974.

42 For an overview of Hanoi's reactions to the Chinese occupation of the Paracels in 1974-1975, see also Chi-kin Lo, *China's Policy toward Territorial Disputes: The Case of the South China Sea Islands*, London and New York: Routledge, 1989, 86–98.

government. As a member of the United Nations, China gave its national promise to comply with international law, but it only does so when it is convenient and supports its goal of subjugating the world and imposing a single-party communist/socialist economic system on the world's population.

In 1988 China once again solved a sovereignty dispute with Vietnam by killing sixty-four and sinking three Vietnamese ships. Naturally there are two sides concerning who shot first, but what is known is that the Vietnamese were not armed and were protecting their national flag previously planted on a minor ocean formation. Unilateral aggression for the purpose of establishing sovereignty issues is not accepted under international law.

INTERNATIONALLY SANCTIONED METHODS OF ACQUIRING OPEN-OCEAN FORMATIONS

There are methods for a nation to acquire additional territory that are sanctioned by international law.[43] The Office of Insular Affairs of the United States commissioned a study on how states may acquire islands as their sovereign territory. The five identified methods were as follows:

Cession

The ceding sovereign transfers its supreme power over the island to the acquiring sovereign. The acquiring sovereign must than take possession of and occupy the island.

Occupation

The island or formation must not be under the supreme power of another sovereign or belonging to anyone (*terra nullius*) and then be occupied and administered by the taking claimant. The administration, to be sufficient, must consist of supervision that exercises the functions of government without disputes being voiced by any other possible claimant.

---

43 A synopsis of the study "Acquisition Process of Insular Areas" may be found at: www.doi.gov/oia/islands/acquisitionprocess.cfm, compiled by Joseph McDermott, OIA, 2003.

Accretion

The island must be created by new geological changes such as the protrusion of a new volcano from the ocean. This process then relates to *terra nullis*, and if the new formation is within the EEZ of a state, that state may claim the new formation.

Subjugation

A sovereign firmly establishes conquest of an island and follows this by formal annexation. Both warring sovereigns must end hostilities by a treaty or merely stop fighting, with the losing sovereign acquiescing to the subjugation.

Prescription

The definition is written in a complex manner. An abbreviated definition in plain English is this:

1. One sovereign takes an island away from a second sovereign by nonhostile action. The donating sovereign must have had a valid claim to the island.
2. The taking sovereign must exercise continuous and undisturbed supreme power over the island for sufficient time for all nations, especially the donating sovereign, to believe that the prescribed island belongs to the taking sovereign "in conformity with international order."
3. Title must be perfected by the taking sovereign through effective and peaceful jurisdiction over the island for a prolonged period.
4. There must be prolonged inaction by other sovereigns that were in a position to contest the claim of the taking sovereign.
5. If no sovereign disputed the claim of a taking sovereign that sovereign would be stopped from contesting the prescribing sovereign's title.[44]

---

44 Joseph McDermott, "Rocks That Cannot Sustain Human Habitation," 93 A.J.I.L. 863, 1999, 877.

CHAPTER 3

China's Internationally Recognized Rights as a Littoral State

———

AS LITTORAL STATES DEVELOPED INDUSTRIALLY and were capable of defending and utilizing the ocean waters out of range of their coastal batteries, they started to name areas of the high seas for legal and treaty identification. Today, the following designations have been accepted into our legal and treaty vocabulary:

* Internal waters
* Territorial waters (seas)
* Contiguous zone
* Exclusive economic zone (EEZ)
* Exclusive fishing zone (EFZ)
* Archipelagic waters
* Continental shelf

INTERNAL WATERS

Internal waters may be considered the sovereign territory of the state in which they exist. Damrosch et al. and Brown quote the 1958 Convention on the Territorial Sea and the Contiguous Zone when defining internal waters as waters wholly or largely surrounded by a state's land territory, as well as sea waters on the landward side of the baseline of the territorial sea.[45, 46]

---

45 Lori Fisler Damrosch, "International Law; Cases and Materials," Fourth Edition, *Derogations from "Commonage" in Favor of Coastal States,* 1390–92.

46 U.N. Convention on the Law of the Sea, 1833 U.N.T.S. 3, U.N. Doc. A/CONF. 62/122, 1982.

States have complete jurisdiction over internal waters, meaning no ship or boat may transit even on an innocent passage. Permission to enter internal waters is identical to the requirements for entry through the state's airports or border crossings. For open-ocean formations, such as those found in the South and East China Seas, the area enclosed by the baseline required by UNCLOS III would be considered "internal waters." Even though China has not filed a baseline supporting its claim to the Scarborough Reef (shoal), it has denied entry to the lagoon surrounded by the reef and is treating the enclosed lagoon as "internal waters" when in fact it is open ocean within the EEZ of the Republic of the Philippines.

Territorial Waters (Seas)

Territorial waters generally extend twelve nautical miles from the low-water line adjacent to the land of littoral states, their internal waters, or the baseline required by UNCLOS III. States have extensive sovereignty rights under international law, and these rights are important in analyzing China's claims of sovereignty over the entire South China Sea.

There are several major areas of concern when administering, such as (1) passage of fishing boats/ships through the territorial waters; (2) passage of boats/ships of foreign states; (3) passage of warships; (4) passage of ships capable of submerged transits; (5) aircraft overflights; and (6) exploration and exploitation of nonliving natural resources. [47]

Passage of Boats/Ships of Foreign States

Customary international law and all subsequent codifications, including UNCLOS III, give substantial weight to freedom of the sea even in territorial waters. All states enjoy the right of innocent passage through the territorial waters of coastal states subject to only a few restrictions. Article 18 of the UNCLOS defines "meaning of passage" with the operative words: *traversing, continuous,* and *expeditious.* The innocent passage of ships does not include

---

47 Ibid.

entering the internal waters or calling at an anchorage (roadstead) or port facility outside the territorial waters of the host state. Exceptions are permitted to protect life and conform to normal navigation channels and anchoring.

Article 19 provides actions that are considered prejudicial to the peace, good order, or security of the coastal state if another state's ship engages in the following selected activities:

(a) any threat or use of force against the host state, its territorial integrity, or political independence, violates international law as embodied in the Charter of the United Nations;

(b) any exercise or practice with weapons of any kind;

(f) the launching, landing or taking on board of any military device;

(g) unloading any commodity or person contrary to regulations of the coastal State;

(j) carrying out of research or survey activities;

(l) any other activity not having a direct bearing on passage.

The previous list is not intended to be comprehensive; it only includes the subsections applicable to the South China Sea disputes. Regretfully, the US Navy has not exercised this right by transiting the claimed territorial seas around the Chinese-claimed formation. The Chinese have made it clear that it does not recognize the right of innocent passage through its territorial seas in discussions within the United Nations. On the other hand, in September of 2015 five People's Liberation Army Navy ships transited the US territorial waters off Alaska in a passage between the Russian Kamchatka peninsula and the American Attu Island. President Obama and Congress did nothing to exercise the same rights in the South China Sea.

Passage of Warships

Warships must comply with laws and regulations of the sovereign state and as defined in Article 19 of the UNCLOS III. While the procedures used in enforcement are not specific, Article 30 appears to deny the host state the right to arrest a warship, but it can require the offending ship to leave its territorial sea immediately. To clarify this issue, even though it is stated in the negative, Article 32 seems to deny immunity from arrest for warships serving in a commercial capacity.[48]

Passage of Ships Capable of Submerged Transits

While all submarines are not warships, all such ships must run on the surface and show their flag while transiting the host state's territorial waters.

Aircraft Overflights

Aircraft in transit over territorial waters must comply with Articles 38 and 39 of UNCLOS. Aircraft must also comply with established International Civil Aviation Organization rules and monitor assigned radio frequencies.[49] This definition becomes critical when analyzing China's recent behavior in establishing Air Defense Identification Zones (ADIZ) beyond the internationally accepted area without consultation with its neighbors; these zones included disputed geographical ocean formations (Japan) and a South Korean island (Socotra Rock).

The United States established ADIZ after the 911 terrorist attack on the World Trade Center in New York; other countries have followed suit, and all, with the exception of China, designated areas that did not overlap their neighbors' ADIZ and did not include land or ocean formations claimed by another nation, and the zones were designated only after consultation with adjacent nations.

China, acting like the bully on the playground, which it is, ignored established norms. Japan and South Korea as of this writing are ignoring the Chinese ADIZ; the US government has done nothing to effectively stop the bully; the American giant led by the Obama administration did not even blink at this

---

48   UNCLOS III 1982; U.N. Convention on the Law of the Sea, 1833 U.N.T.S. 3, U.N. Doc. A/CONF. 62/122, 1982.

49   Ibid.

belligerent act. True, a few planes were sent to transit the illegal ADIZ, but China has not backed down from its claim to add territorial air space control without consent of its neighbors. The Japanese civilian flights continue to transit the illegal ADIZ, but it appears the United States has forgotten the incident and is not applying pressure on China to rescind the ADIZ. The US foreign policy continues as probably predicted by China; the American giant grunts a little in the beginning and then quickly goes back to sleep.

Additionally, Japan filed a complaint with the International Civil Aviation Organization, an organization of the UN, with support from Australia, the Philippines, the United Kingdom of Great Britain, and the United States. The Chinese objected vehemently, so its lapdog, the UN, did nothing to stop the bully.

EXPLORATION AND EXPLOITATION OF NONLIVING NATURAL RESOURCES

The sovereignty of a coastal state extends to and includes its territorial sea. Judge Huber's dicta in the Island of Palmas case stated: "Territorial sovereignty…involves the exclusive right to display the activities of a state. And: Sovereignty…signifies…independence in regard to a portion of the globe is the right to exercise therein, to the exclusion of any other State, the functions of a State." The South China Sea dispute is not only a sovereignty issue but also an issue of whether a state may control the resources of the high seas *without* complying with the terms of the convention.

CONTIGUOUS WATERS

Contiguous waters are zones of the high seas abutting the territorial waters of a state. States are limited to twenty-four nautical miles maximum by UNCLOS III, twelve for a territorial sea and twelve for a contiguous zone, measured from the state's baseline as filed with the United Nations.[50] The purpose of

---

50 The "filing" requirement will be discussed later because the People's Republic of China filed a nonconforming baseline, and the United Nations apparently has no capability to correct the inappropriate filing.

the contiguous zone is to provide an additional buffer for the host state to protect its sovereignty. The specific powers of a state in its contiguous waters are severely limited by UNCLOS III.

Article 33(1) provides for the coastal state to pass and promulgate laws and regulations to control (1) customs, (2) fiscal, (3) immigration, or (4) sanitary laws for its territorial waters. The contiguous zone only provides an additional area of the high seas to prevent foreign states from violating customs, fiscal, immigration, or sanitary laws and regulations of the host state.

Exclusive Economic Zone

Moving seaward, the exclusive economic zone (EEZ) is beyond and adjacent to the territorial sea out to two hundred nautical miles from the coastal nations' baselines. Properly filing a baseline allows sovereign rights over all living and nonliving natural resources in the water, seabed, and the seabed subsoil subject to the restriction delineated in Part V of UNCLOS III. The restrictions that are applicable to South China Sea disputes concern utilization of living resources. Specifically, a sovereign has the right to impose a fishing license requirement on foreign fishermen that will protect its natural resources from being overfished.

In reference to the South China Sea disputes, the protection of coral reefs and fishing are important. On the other hand, in these disputes, no exclusive sovereign has been recognized by all claimant nations, and no formations have been classified as "islands." Malaysia has unilaterally classified Swallow Reef as an island even though it does not qualify as an island in accordance with UNCLOS III Article 121(3).[51] Swallow Reef has a runway capable of taking aircraft onboard the reef. It is approximately 146 nautical miles from Malaysia and also supports a light as an aide to navigation. Malaysia has designated this reef an island and has claimed territorial seas around the reef. Apparently, to push their claim of sovereignty, they have established a fifteen-room resort and have planted trees. The water, food, and fuel requirements remain a problem; all supplies must be transported to Swallow Reef by ship, boat, or

---

51 Ibid.

plane. It is an isolated, submerged coral atoll with a man-made island covering approximately six hectares. The estimated size is 7.3 kilometers by 2.2 kilometers with safe anchorage and fixed mooring buoys.

Swallow Reef was the site of the Labuan International Maritime Challenges in May 2003. The People's Republic of China protested the games and tried to bully Malaysia into canceling the event. The games were not canceled. Malaysia has only claimed a "territorial sea" around the reef, probably realizing it would never qualify as an island. Perhaps the Malaysian leaders are acting rationally and, notwithstanding the destruction of a large part of the coral reef, are exercising administration and control over Malaysia's territorial sea and not trying to bully its neighbor to believe it has rights beyond the territorial sea and a contiguous zone.

EXCLUSIVE FISHING ZONE

The EFZ, for all practical and legal purposes, has merged with the EEZ. Brown discussed the history of the exclusive fishing zone and how it was included in UNCLOS III.[52] These two zones may be integrated in future versions of the Law of the Sea. They appear redundant as written in UNCLOS III.

ARCHIPELAGIC WATERS

Controversy riddled international law until the states could agree on how to measure the breadth of their territorial waters. The concept of three nautical miles and other widths did not resolve the issues until the additional concept of a baseline was introduced by the United Nations. Once a workable definition of a nation's baseline was provided by UNCLOS III, all nations could file charts with their baselines delineated. The problem of how to measure a baseline for archipelagic states then became a problem. As Brown noted, prior to UNCLOS III, much work had already been accomplished in defining an archipelagic state and its associated baseline. Articles 46 and 47

---

52 Brown.

of UNCLOS III provide the geometry for defining an archipelagic state's baseline.[53]

Furtado also identified problems associated with defining baselines for coastal states that are sovereign over islands such as China and the United States. He used the Philippine definition of archipelagic as being similar in nature to internal waters of a nation.[54] No one appears to have identified an accepted procedure for determining baselines for islands belonging to a state that is not archipelagic. The only possible conclusion may be to follow the examples of other nonarchipelagic states and treat their islands over which these nations have sovereignty the same as the United States did for the Hawaiian Island chain and China does over Taiwan and Hainan by drawing the baselines as if they were part of the mainland. Since the People's Republic of China is not an archipelagic state, their island baselines do not come under the archipelagic exceptions.

CONTINENTAL SHELF

The continental shelf is defined as a natural prolongation of a nation's land territory to the outer edge of the continental margin. I would have preferred UNCLOS did not include Part VI Continental Shelf in UNCLOS III. An EEZ with a maximum breadth of two hundred nautical miles from a nation's baseline covers an extensive body of water, seabed, and subsoil and would appear sufficient to satisfy the needs of even the most demanding nation. Defining the limits of a continental shelf is difficult and in some cases requires extensive use of scientific analysis.

For example, Article 76 (4)(a)(i) of UNCLOS III requires the claiming nation to determine the thickness of sedimentary rocks and prove that its origination is connected to the mainland or an island. This can only be done by use of seismic experimentation or coring. Both methods are expensive and time consuming.[55] In addition to the difficulty in defining the limits of the continental shelf, a question remains as to how much encroachment of the high seas is enough.

---

53 Ibid.

54 Xavier Furtado, "International Law and the Dispute over the Spratly Islands: Whither UNCLOS?" *Contemporary Southeast Asia*, Vol. 21, No. 3, 1999.

55 UNCLOS III.

CHAPTER 4

The Future of Ocean Transit Rights of the South China Sea Depends on How International Law Defines an Island, and Why Care?

————

IF THIS BOOK WERE ABOUT the Gobi or Sahara deserts, there would be no questioning of the definition for rocks, land, and coral, and there should be no dispute over the definition concerning the use of these terms in UNCLOS III. It seems logical that when the drafting nations' representatives met, they decided to use the normal, everyday definitions for such common words without providing alternatives.

Reading UNCLOS III as a whole, there is no reason to distinguish among land masses, rocks, or coral. If one grounds his ship or boat on any one of these, the results are the same. On the other hand, land (dirt, soil) may provide for crops and be the basis for satisfying the "sustain human habitation" requirements for the definition of an island that rate an EEZ and continental shelf.

The People's Republic of China has not been consistent with its use of terms designating sovereignty of ocean areas as delineated earlier. For example, in 2014 the Chinese placed the HD-981 mobile oil drilling rig seventeen miles south of the Paracel Islands. Using this geographical location, the Chinese minister of foreign affairs stated that China had the right to drill at this location because it would be located on the "continental shelf" extending to the south of the Paracel Islands.[56]

---

56 Hilary Whiteman, "How an Oil Rig Sparked Anti-China Riots in Vietnam," accessed at http://www.cnn.com/2014/05/19/world/asia/china-vietna-islands-oil-rig-explainr/index.html.

To use the continental shelf connected to the Paracel Islands as a legitimate basis for exploiting subsoil hydrocarbon deposits, China would have to be the recognized sovereign of the Paracel Islands, and it would also have to have filed a baseline around the island with the United Nations, and the formation would have to qualify as an "island."

The Chinese are not the recognized sovereign of the Paracel Islands internationally, notwithstanding their continuous propaganda claiming the formation. Vietnam has constantly objected to their invasion of the Paracels since 1974, but the world and the United States did not listen. To complicate matters, the Chinese filed a fraudulent baseline with the United Nations for the Paracels, and the United Nations did nothing when Vietnam filed a complaint concerning nonconformance of the filing.

This is important because to determine rights to underground resources on ocean beds requires proper conforming baselines as specified in UNCLOS III. If China is recognized as the sovereign of the Paracel Islands and one of the formations is classified as an island in accordance with UNCLOS III, then China would be correct in claiming that it had a valid claim to the substrata, open-ocean hydrocarbons where they position the HD-981.

China's argument concerning the placement of HD-981 on the continental shelf emanating from the Paracel Islands would only be legitimate if sovereignty over the Paracel Islands was determined by adjudication or bilateral agreement in view of the Vietnamese claims to the same islands. The next major and perhaps insurmountable decision would have to be made on whether Woody Island is an island capable of sustaining human habitation or an economic life of its own.

It should be no surprise to students of the United Nations Law of the Sea (UNCLOS III) and the United States why the Chinese are converting islets, rocks, and submerged formations in the South China Sea to quasi "islands." Since the United Nations has been ineffective in policing the terms of UNCLOS III, in the near future China will claim these "islands" they have created are the foundation for an announcement to the world that each of the quasi islands rates its own exclusive economic zone (EEZ), which now includes an exclusive fishing zone (EFZ) and attached continental shelf.

To understand the Chinese reasoning for attempting to convince the world their quasi islands should be treated as islands as defined by UNCLOS III, visualize, hypothetically, a new ocean formation appearing in the middle of the doldrums area of the Pacific Ocean, say, on the equator at the 120th degree of west longitude. Within days of its formation, presume it is discovered by a passing seaman, and the seaman claims it in the name of his country, Guatemala. Guatemala passes the requisite legislation and claims this new insular area based on occupation of *terra nullis* and discovery and subsequently files the necessary documents with the United Nations delineating a baseline and EEZ. It is named Isla Bolivar. No other state challenges Guatemala's sovereignty over Isla Bolivar, and all newly printed Guatemalan maps and other nations' mapping services indicate Isla Bolivar as Guatemalan. These maps are subsequently delivered to all members of the General Assembly of the United Nations and filed with the United Nations.

The archipelagic state of Kiribati is due west of Isla Bolivar and the home of the best albacore tuna in the world. For years tuna fishermen paid the government of Kiribati large sums of money to fish for the prized long-fin tuna in their EEZ. Changes in climate conditions have caused the albacore to migrate away from the Kiribati Islands to the waters around Isla Bolivar. Guatemala institutes a fishing license for its EEZ around Isla Bolivar at a cost of $100,000 USD per calendar year and a surcharge based on the catch tonnage. The countries that fish albacore—United States, Canada, Japan, and Spain—protest Guatemala's right to demand the licenses based on their opinion that Isla Bolivar is not an island but a rock.

Guatemala will add approximately $6 million USD to their gross national product, and the price of albacore in Japan will become exorbitant if Guatemala prevails in having the United Nations recognize Isla Bolivar as an Article 121(1), (2), and (3) island. Prior to the tuna migration, Japan had unlimited fishing rights around Kiribati but now must pay Guatemala for their catch.

Japan and Guatemala have been unable to resolve their differences, so they have submitted their dispute to a third party for resolution in accordance with UNCLOS III, Part XV: *Settlement of Disputes.*

While Isla Bolivar is a hypothetical problem, Charney provided an excellent summary of disputes that would help resolve the issue once the International Court of Justice provides a definitive answer to the Philippine-China dispute over sovereignty of the Scarborough Reef.[57] The Guatemalan hypothetical is simple to decide for the same reasons the Paracel, Spratly, and Scarborough Reef issues are difficult. There is no question Isla Bolivar is *terra nullis*; there is no question of who discovered the formation; and there is no question on Guatemala's continuous administration of the formation. The only remaining issue is whether the formation is an island as defined in Article 121(3) of UNCLOS (1982). The issues presented by the Philippines concerning China's claims are unclear and are made more so by the physical fact that Scarborough Reef is nothing more than a few rocks jutting out of the water (in high seas) in the South China Sea but located in the Philippine EEZ.

The arbitral tribunal between the Philippines and China is different than the Guatemalan position. First, the Philippines wants Scarborough Reef (shoal) to be defined as a "rock," which would limit a future dispute over sovereignty of territorial waters of 452.4 nautical miles.[2] On the other hand, if the tribunal decides that Scarborough Reef is an "island," the dispute would be over 125,664 nautical miles.[2]

Based on readings of the filed documents, it appears the tribunal will be addressing the issue of sovereignty based on the information provided by the foreign affairs secretary of the Philippines, Albert del Rosario, by confirming the memorandum submitted to the arbitral panel containing forty maps. These maps would not have been necessary if the only issue was whether to label it a rock or an island. Whatever decision the tribunal makes, the world should listen because of the quality of the members hearing the dispute.

High Seas

There has always been competition between those who would divide the world's high seas among nations and those who would fight to keep the high

---

57 Jonathan I. Charney, *Rocks That Cannot Sustain Human Habitation*, 93 A.J.I.L. 863, 877, 1999.

seas free from all sovereignty claims. N. J. Schrijver lauded UNCLOS III for stemming the "rush of coastal States to claim more of the sea" and denigrate what remains of the principle of the freedom of the high seas.[58]

The first encroachment of the high seas was the defining of territorial waters and nations claiming those waters. Damrosch, Henkin, Pugh, Schachter, and Smit from Columbia University, citing Walker, quoted a maxim of the early eighteenth-century Dutch jurist Bynkershoek that provided the basis for the three-nautical-mile rule for a nation's territorial waters as being the range of coastal cannons.

Damrosch et al. go on to further define the limits of territorial waters by citing the 1906 edition of the *Moore Digest of International Law*, where in 1793 the United States set its territorial waters at one sea league. France and the United Kingdom of Great Britain and Northern Ireland (hereinafter Great Britain) agreed with the US position, and the three-nautical-mile territorial sea was the standard used in subsequent court cases between these nations concerning prizes of war taken at sea.[59, 60]

The basis for the US decision to set territorial waters at three nautical miles could have been either the English or French system of measurements. The English defined a league as approximately three land miles (5,280 feet per mile), which was intended to be an hour's walk. The French set the *lieue marine* at 5,556 meters (which was very close to the 5,486.4 meters, which equals three nautical miles). The United States Court of Appeals for the Second Circuit (in Re: Air Crash Off Long Island, New York, on July 17, 1996) provided an excellent analysis of the history of definitions for territorial waters and high seas.

In reference to the Isla Bolivar hypothetical, Guatemala claims a territorial sea of twelve nautical miles and an EEZ diameter of four hundred nautical miles from the edge of the territorial sea. When Guatemala ratified UNCLOS

---

58 N. J. Schrijver, "The Law of the Sea: Extension of Control over Marine Resource," *Planet Ocean*, 189, 1995.

59 Damrosch, Henkin, Pugh, Schachter, Smit, *International Law*, 1393, West Group, American Casebook Series, 2001.

60 Walker, *Territorial Waters: The Cannon Shot Rule*, 22 Brit.Y.B.I.L. 210, 213–22, 1945.

on November 2, 1997, it did not specify the outer limits for its continental shelf, nor did it delineate a contiguous zone.[61]

If Guatemala prevails in the litigation over our hypothetical formation, Isla Bolivar, it will have 125,664 square nautical miles of EEZ, which would include an area of 452.4 square nautical miles of territorial seas. Should Japan prevail, Guatemala will only have the territorial sea under her administrative control. The area lost would be slightly smaller than the state of Montana. More important would be Guatemala's loss of Japanese revenue it would have collected for the fishing license fees. This begs the question, what would China gain if the United Nations tribunal decided against the Philippines and any other challenger to the Chinese claim that the quasi islands rate their own EEZs?

SUBMERGED CORAL REEFS

There are three types of submerged coral reefs: those within the territorial seas of a state, those within the EEZ of a nation, and those found on the high seas.

The formations found under the territorial seas of a nation present no problems in international law. Article 2 of UNCLOS III provides sovereignty of the submerged reef subject to UNCLOS III and other rules of international law. Submerged coral reefs found within a nation's EEZ may be exploited by the nation subject to international agreements specifically protective of coral and the environment. For example, the UN Conference on Environment and Development (UNCED) Article 17.1 (d) requires nations to provide for sustainable use and conservation of marine living resources under the nation's jurisdiction. Submerged coral reefs have no effect on establishing a nation's baseline for determining its territorial seas.

Apparently, the People's Republic of China and Vietnam do not believe this mandate applies to them. The destruction of coral reefs to build military structures violates UNCED and UNCLOS III. As an additional example of China's disregard for the environment, when Chinese fishermen were caught

---

61 United Nations, *Maritime Claims,* Legislation and Treaties, accessed at http://www.un.org/Depts/los/LGISLATIONANDTREATIES/laims.htm on July 17, 2012.

with boatloads of soft coral and dynamite, Beijing protected the fishermen by claiming the Philippine sailors mistook fishing baskets for coral. Eleven days after the first incident, the Philippines confiscated other Chinese fishing boats with coral and dynamite on board. The People's Republic changed tack and, in place of arguing the innocence of the Chinese fishermen, attacked the Philippines for creating new trouble in the South China Sea.

SUBMERGED LAND

Other names for submerged lands are sea floor, sea mountain, underwater volcano, and continental shelf. These formations are subject to the same protection as submerged coral, and they also have no effect on establishing a nation's baseline. This is true even if China builds up the submerged formation artificially.

SHOALS

A shoal formation is not defined as separate from submerged coral or land; however, years at sea have led me to believe that a shoal is nothing more than submerged coral, which is a hazard to navigation. For example, the term *rocks and shoals* for men who go to sea refers to the danger of grounding and losing one's ship. The British Hydrographic Office plots the formation disputed by the Philippines and China as "Scarborough Reef"; however, on other charts it is plotted as Scarborough Shoal.

Shoals have no effect on establishing a nation's baseline unless they are in the immediate vicinity of an island or the low-water tide line of a littoral nation.

BANKS

Banks are similar to shoals but are generally not considered a danger to navigation. This is purely an arbitrary definition based only on usage by mariners, but it will do for the purpose of this book because banks have no effect on establishing a nation's baseline.

The *Consolidated Glossary* supporting UNCLOS does provide the following: "An elevation of the sea floor located on a continental (or an island) shelf, over which the depth of water is relatively shallow. And a shallow area of shifting sand, gravel, mud, etc. as a sand bank, mud bank, etc. usually constituting a danger to navigation and occurring in relatively shallow waters."

BREAKERS

Breakers, on the other hand, may have a definite impact on determining a baseline. Breakers are marked with a "Br" on Admiralty Charts. The issue is whether a breaker is a low-tide elevation as defined in UNCLOS III. Resolving the difference between a low-tide elevation and a reef would seem to depend on whether or not the formation, against which the waves and surges were breaking, remained above the water at low tide.

Most mariners opt for defining the formation as a low-tide elevation if on a calm day with no surges or waves, the formation is above water at low tide and underwater at high tide. This is an important issue to be resolved by archipelagic states trying to define their baselines. For example, if the formation is above water at high tide, then it is no longer a low-tide elevation and becomes a formation that is not defined in UNCLOS III. If it is underwater at low tide, it becomes a submerged rock, coral, or land and has no impact on defining a baseline. This brings up the definition of "rocks, land, and coral."

LOW-TIDE ELEVATIONS

UNCLOS III uses only "land" in its definition for a low-tide elevation in Article 13. Did the members of the convention intend to exclude rock or coral formations that satisfied the definition of a low-tide elevation from baseline formation criteria? If they so intended, what would a court/tribunal do with a rock formation that had accumulated a small quantity of dirt or guano on its surface? Does a quantity of dirt make the rock land? The same question would apply to a low-tide coral elevation. Is this not how some larger islands were formed in the South Pacific?

The members of the convention of UNCLOS III seemed intent on extending the reach of nations so they could exploit more and more of the high seas. They could have stopped at the mainland coast or the low-water tide line of a fringing reef of an island without reaching out for greater breadth of the high seas. They wrote the convention articles so the states would have all the high seas they could justify. It would follow that it makes no difference whether the low-water tide elevation is formed by rock, land, coral, or sand as demonstrated by China laying claim to Scarborough Reef 440 nautical miles from its mainland and 124 nautical miles from the Philippines and within its EEZ.

CORAL REEFS

UNCLOS III did not provide a definition for coral reefs and thus created major difficulties for nations making claims to the various formations in the South China Sea. One can define a coral reef starting with what it is not. It is not a submerged rock, islet, bank, or shoal but could possibly be a low-tide elevation. It is also not an island if it cannot sustain human habitation or an economic life of its own.

As noted herein before, the United Nations did, however, provide definitions for use with the Convention on the Law of the Sea. The following are the definitions provided in reference to reefs:

*   Reef. A mass of rock or coral which either reaches close to the sea surface or is exposed at low tide.
*   Drying reef. That part of a reef which is above water at low tide but submerged at high tide.
*   Fringing reef. A reef attached directly to the shore or continental land mass, or located in their immediate vicinity.
*   Islands on atolls. In the case of islands situated on atolls or of islands having fringing reefs, the baseline...is seaward low-water line of the reef, as shown by the appropriate symbol on charts officially recognized by the coastal State[62].

---

62 UNCLOS III

Geologically, coral reefs are divided into three groups: (1) fringing reefs; (2) barrier reefs; and (3) atolls. Reefs are limestone formations produced by living organisms and found in tropical waters generally between thirty degrees North and South latitudes no deeper than thirty meters below the surface of the ocean in water no colder than twenty-two degrees Celsius. Fringing reefs are as defined earlier but with the additional requirement that they be exposed at low tide. Barrier reefs, not mentioned in UNCLOS III or the *Glossary*, are separated from the shoreline by a deep lagoon or surround a lagoon in mid-ocean that has an island or islet in its center. An atoll is a reef surrounding a lagoon that does not have an island or islet in its center.[63]

ISLETS

These definitions do not provide a name or status for a formation that is above the high-water tide line but is not an island—as written, the only alternative is "rock." As noted before, what if the rock acquires topsoil or guano and can support some small amounts of vegetation and palm trees but does not have sufficient fresh water to support human life? The formation becomes a hybrid without classification. Mariners, as a matter of practice, refer to these hybrids as coral reefs and maybe even islands. Charts consulted for this book include many such examples. What if a number of these coral reef hybrids cluster in a given area of the high seas? Does a cluster have more international legal weight than one lonely formation in the doldrums of the Pacific?

So there it is—a coral, rock, land formation that is not an island and above the high-water tide line has no legal status, but the ramifications these nondefined formations will have on any tribunals decision related to the disputes over them in the South China Sea is enormous.

Perhaps they should be referred to as "islets." The charts consulted for this book do list a few formations as "islets." One of the references in the literature is "Marion Islets." Marion Islets cannot be found on the appropriate admiralty chart. Common usage would define islets as small islands, but this is of no value in establishing baselines, nor is islet defined in the *Consolidated*

---

63   J. A. Fagerstrom, *The Evolution of Reef Coral*, 1987.

Glossary.[64] Judge Oda in his separate opinion in *Qatar v. Bahrain* used the terms *small island* and *islet* to refer to these formations. His separate opinion and its ramifications on this issue will be discussed in detail later.[65]

Rocks

Even though the term *rock* is used in defining whether or not a formation may or may not be the basis for claim of an exclusive economic zone (EEZ), rock is not defined in the UNLOS III. Article 121(3) reads: "Regime of Islands: Rocks which cannot sustain human habitation or economic life of their own shall have no exclusive economic zone or continental shelf."

The only reference to rocks is a formation that is above the high-water tide level, which would include sandbars and organically formed reefs. The drafters of Article 121 must have intended all formations above the high-water tide elevation because not including them would eliminate the majority of formations that exist above the high-water tide elevations, such as reefs and sand islands, which are prevalent in the South China Sea.

Islands

Articles 121(1) and 121(3) of UNCLOS III define what a sovereign of an island is entitled to with some specificity. This definition is critical in determining the sovereignty of an ocean formation. There appears to be no problem with defining a formation that is constantly above the high-water tide line,

---

64 Glossary of Technical Terns, in *Continental Shelf Limits: The Scientific and Legal Interface* 321-30 (PeterJ. Cook & Chris M. Carleton eds., 2000). Besides the Consolidated Glossary, supra note 77, Annex 1, contains various sources. See Am. Geological Inst., *Dictionary of Geological Terms* (Robert L. Bates & Julia A. Jackson eds., 3d ed. 1984); Am. Geological Inst., *Glossary of Geology* (Julia A. Jackson ed., 4th ed. 1997); and Ass'n For Geographic Info. & Edinburgh Univ., *Online Dictionary* (1996, rev. 2003), available at www.agi.org.uk/public/gis.resources/index.htm (last visited Feb. 10, 2003; server failure noted June 1, 2008). 79. See supra note 7 and accompanying text.

65 "Qatar & Bahrain, Case Concerning Maritime Delimitation & Territorial Question Between," UN DL 202 *World Court Digest*, 2001.

but Article 121(3) adds the requirement that the formation be able to sustain human habitation or an economic life of its own.

The *Consolidated Glossary*, Article 41, eliminates artificial islands, installations, and structures as having territorial seas of their own, and their presence does not affect the delimitation of the territorial seas, the exclusive economic zones, or the continental shelves.[66]

Whiting used strong language on this issue, favoring the nations that want to limit incursion and control of the high seas, but his logic is confusing. For example, Whiting wrote, "Article 60(8) clearly states that artificial islands...will not affect the delimitation of the exclusive economic zone... although the structures may strengthen (the claimants)...through use of the island."[67] This conclusion is confusing. If the use of artificial structures does not affect the EEZ, it would mean it prevents the formation from being classified as an Article 121(3) island. On the other hand, the second half of the sentence concerning strengthening the claimants' uses (administrative control?) of the island is a contrary conclusion unless he was referring to a sovereignty issue.

Several nations have built artificial structures on high-tide elevations, nonisland reefs, and even submerged reefs in the Spratly and Paracel islands. These structures, no matter how substantial, do not qualify the formation as an island unless the formation was an "island" before construction. Judge Oda touched briefly on this issue in his dissent in *Qatar v. Bahrain* by politely admonishing the majority for not being more circumspect in handing down its decision on islands and high-tide elevations (rocks). Judge Oda believed that the legal status of structures built on reefs and low-tide elevations would be reserved for future discussions. He was correct—all nations that transit the South China Sea will have a stake in the Chinese claim to all the formations in this sea if their artificial structures allow China to claim internal water, territorial waters, and economic exclusion zones around these artificial structures.

---

66 *Consolidated Glossary of Technical Terms.*
67 David Whiting, "The Spratly Islands Dispute and the Law of the Sea," *Denver Journal of International Law & Politics*, 26, 897, 1998.

A difficulty in providing a working definition for the term *island* is the general misuse of the term in maritime literature. For example, the *Absolute Astronomy Encyclopedia* purports to provide facts and information on the Spratly Islands. They list the coordinates of the Spratlys at 8 degrees, 38 minutes north, and 111 degrees, 55 minutes east. This is not the center of the Spratlys; it is the location of Spratly Island. The *Encyclopedia* goes on to state that the islands contain no arable land and have no indigenous inhabitants; yet twenty of the islands, including Itu Aba, are considered to be able to sustain human life. The last statement is of concern because the writer refers to twenty reefs and islets as "islands" and claims that they may be able to sustain human life with no explanation of how humans would survive since there is no arable land, no source of fresh water other than some small wells and occasional tropical rains, and no source of fuel.

Even named formations that remain above the water at high tide have traditionally been referred to as islands. True, UNCLOS III defines any formation existing above high tide as an island, and because it does so, one must then separate those that conform to the definition of Article 121(3) and those that do not. Perhaps a solution to this confusion would be to follow Judge Oda's lead and refer to islands that do not conform to Article 121(3) as islets.

It will be argued later that there are no formations that qualify as islands in the South China Sea as defined in UNCLOS Article 121(3). And for the purpose of this analysis, an assumption is made that the PRC has sovereignty over these formations. The issue then becomes, with sovereignty established, what rights does the PRC have over the formations that are not "islands"?

I believe Judge Oda in his separate opinion in *Qatar v. Bahrain* touched on this subject tangentially. In paragraph 7 he focused on the issue of the importance of low-tide elevations and the impact of that importance when the territorial sea limit was extended from three to twelve nautical miles. Then, as if to follow the discussion of high-tide elevations, he offered the following in paragraph 8:

> The provisions on islands in the 1982 United Nations Convention on the Law of the Sea come from the 1930 text of the Hague Codification Conference and the 1958 Convention on the Territorial sea. But small

islands and islets did not receive specific attention and the provision on islands in general would have applied. In UNCLOS III there were some efforts, although at an unofficial level, to define "island" more cautiously so that the title granted under the 1958 Convention would not extend to small islands or islets. These efforts did not produce any clear result. I wish to mention this, as I have some doubts as to whether Article 121 concerning the regime of island of the 1982 United Nations Convention which does not refer to islets or small islands may as a whole be considered the customary international law in the age when the 12 mile territorial sea prevails.[68]

Judge Oda addressed low-tide elevations in paragraph 7 of his separate opinion, and he referred to islands in paragraph 8 as in, "The provisions on islands in the 1982." He then used the term "small islands and islets" but did not define them. I do believe that Judge Oda was referring to islets as defined earlier as formations remaining above the high-water tide line that do not qualify as islands (rocks). Note how he wrote, "But small islands and islets did not receive specific attention." Logically there are no other formations to which he would be referring. He provided further writings that supported this position by making reference to Article 121(3) of UNCLOS III as "some efforts...to define 'island' more cautiously so that the title granted under the 1958 convention would not extend to small islands or islets."

UNCLOS III does in fact restrict the 1958 Convention on the Territorial Sea by requiring islands to support human habitation or an economic life of their own.. This article does restrict islets and formations from being defined as "islands," and therefore a sovereign is not able to sustain a claim for an exclusive economic zone and is limited to a defined territorial sea.

Judge Oda concluded paragraph 8 with an interesting observation. He doubted that Article 121 would become customary international law in the age of twelve-mile territorial seas because it did not define the effect of "islets or small islands" nor include them in the article. The "effect" to which he referred is the recognition of an exclusive economic zone around an island.

---

68   *Qatar & Bahrain.*

To better understand his position, one needs to refer to his comparison of the effect of high-tide elevations on baselines using a three-mile territorial sea and a twelve-mile territorial sea. He even wrote in paragraph 7 that this issue had been given very little thought in academic and judicial circles.

Scott Snyder, writing for the United States Institute of Peace (USIP), took the position that the People's Republic of China's baseline around the Paracels deviated from conventional practices, and the United States would probably dispute the Chinese baseline. (The United Nations failed to take up this issue, allowing China to prevail without argument.) Snyder based his conclusion on the requirement that only archipelagic states may draw baselines around islands. He does not address the issue that none of the Paracels are islands but are mere islets (rocks) and are only entitled to a territorial sea at best.[69]

Three years later in 1998, Whiting carried on with the same theme by questioning how the People's Republic of China, or any claimant, would draw a baseline in the Spratlys conforming to Article 47. Whiting focused on the land-to-water ratio as was used in the analysis previously discussed.

Judge Oda's reservation on the issue of small islands and islets (hereinafter referred to as "islets") is on point for the issues of baseline determination in the Paracel and Spratly islands.

TREATMENT OF ISLETS IN REFERENCE TO BASELINE DETERMINATION

The members of the convention of UNCLOS III set out in clear terms how to include or exclude low-tide elevations when determining baselines. Article 13 is clear and to the point. If a low-tide elevation is within the territorial sea of an island or mainland, the baseline is extended to encompass the formation. If it is not within the territorial sea of an island or mainland, it is not.

---

69   Scott Snyder, *The South China Sea Dispute Prospects for Preventive Diplomacy*, United States Institute of Peace, 1995, http://www.usip.org/pubs/specialreports/early/snyder/South_China_Sea, accessed on June 22, 2006.

Islands have their own territorial sea, contiguous zone, and exclusive economic zone, and if appropriate, the sovereign of an island may extend its control over the island's continental shelf.

The islets in the South China Sea are all located on the high seas. An in-depth analysis of which formations may or may not qualify as islands in accordance with Article 121 will eventually have to be adjudicated by a United Nations tribunal or the International Court of Justice. For now, please assume that all formations are islets, reefs, low-tide elevations, banks, shoals, or mounts. The Philippines versus the People's Republic of China arbitration may resolve this issue for some formations.

As defined earlier, a low-tide elevation midocean has no territorial sea. True, it is subject to the administration of a sovereign, but the sovereign will have no rights other than the surface of the rock or coral exposed at low tide. But consider what rights a sovereign has over an islet. The majority of the court in *Qatar v. Bahrain* emphasized the difference between low-tide elevations and islands and, specifically, the inability of a low-tide elevation situated beyond the territorial sea of a nation not having a territorial sea of its own. This difference was the basis for the court's finding that a low-tide elevation does not generate the same rights as islands or other territories with regard to appropriations by a nation.

Judge Oda was not so sure; he questioned whether sovereignty over an islet or a low-tide elevation may be acquired through appropriation by a nation and the extent of the territorial sea or the boundary of the territorial sea. The critical point of both Judge Oda's doubt and the court's finding is that appropriation of islets and low-tide elevations was not addressed for those formations found on the high seas.

In 1929 a group of five experts was appointed at the behest of the League of Nations to review input from nations on the issue of the effect of islands on territorial seas and to evaluate what parameters would constitute an island. These experts were supposedly picked because they possessed a wide knowledge of international legal practice, legal precedents, and scientific data relating to the questions of territorial sea boundaries and islands.

The consensus of the group as reported to the Conference for the Codification of International Law convened at The Hague on March 13, 1930, included the following:

- Certain islands have their own territorial sea.
- An island permanently above water at high tide has its own territorial sea.
- An island above water only at low tide may be taken into account in determining baselines.

What is now referred to as a low-tide elevation in UNCLOS III was merely an island in 1929.

As stated herein, Judge Oda, in his separate opinion, characterized UNCLOS III as defining islands "more cautiously so that the title granted under the 1958 convention would not extend to small islands or islets." Using this more restrictive definition and following Judge Oda's trend, islets cannot rise to the level of importance of an island.

Extrapolating from Judge Oda's writing, if an islet cannot support human life or an economic life of its own, it does not deserve a territorial sea of its own. Perhaps the more restrictive definition of island provides a better understanding of the race in the South China Sea to station troops, conduct athletic games, build structures, place monuments, remove others' monuments, and continuously proclaim sovereignty over the formations. By so doing, states are attempting to transform islets into islands by sheer force, artificial structures, and propaganda.

With the exception of Itu Aba (Taiping Island), all formations should be classified as "islets." Itu Aba, along with Woody Island, satisfy some of the requirements for being classified as an UNCLOS III island; these formations have fresh-water wells, which would assist in classifying this formation as an island.

In 2006 approximately forty-seven of the South China Sea formations of an estimated sixty possible islets were occupied by the contesting nations; this is a high percentage of occupation for nonproductive ocean dots. Each garrison must be provided with food and water merely to survive. Perhaps the only reason for so doing would be to convince any potential tribunal adjudicating the sovereignty issues of these formations that the islets could sustain human life and therefore qualify as islands.

Charney, as noted previously, makes an excellent argument that artificially improving an islet should transmute an islet to an island. His argument, however, is based on an assumption that will draw loud dissenting voices from most readers of law. Charney overcomes the Article 121(1) requirement that an island be a "naturally formed area of land, which is above water at high tide" by eliminating the "natural" requirement for Article 121(3). He does this by stating on page 867 that "the text of paragraph 3 does not specify that the conditions set out there must also exist naturally."

On the other hand, there is no language bifurcating subsection 121(1) from 121(3). Judge Vereshchetin in his declaration in *Qatar v. Bahrain* stressed the inappropriateness of the alleged attempts by both Qatar and Bahrain to artificially change the upper part of a "tiny maritime feature" so it would be considered an island. Judge Vereshchetin also makes his voice heard in support of determining effects on baselines and sovereignty of formations before any artificial changes are made to the formation and not vice versa. He does, however, in a footnote, agree that resources beyond the territorial sea should not be used to establish the basis for "an economic life on its own" since the rights to such resources is the crux of the issue.

This was one of the most important dicta from the case; Judge Vereshchetin required that the sovereignty issue be decided without considering any resources (water, food, fuel) that do not naturally originate on the disputed formation.

E. D. Brown refers to the Resolution of the Imperial Conference 1923 for support that UNCLOS III intended to include "natural" in Article 121(3). Brown quotes paragraph 22 of the explanatory memorandum, which the conference had before it, as follows:

The phrase "capable of use or habitation" has been adopted as a compromise. It is intended that the words "capable of use" should mean capable, without artificial addition, of being used throughout all seasons for some definite commercial or defense purpose, and that "capable of habitation" should mean capable, without artificial addition, of permanent human habitation.[70]

Brown, as did Judge Oda, criticizes UNCLOS III for not adding additional language such as "without artificial addition" to Article 121(3) (Brown, 1994). Dr. Dubner uses E. D. Brown's work in his *Temple International and Comparative Law Journal* article on the definition of islands. Dr. Dubner writes on page 305, "It appears that the rocks may have an economic life of their own." He does not provide an explanation of how these rocks may have an economic life of their own.[71]

Christopher Joyner does not focus on the issue of what is an Article 121(3) island but does make a blanket statement to the effect that formations in the Spratly Islands are too small to support human settlement independently and few have fresh water or any significant land-based resources. He does continue his excellent paper by assuming the Spratly formations may serve as the basis for exclusive jurisdiction over waters and resources, which contradicts his statement concerning the lack of fresh water and significant land-based resources and conflicts with the definitions found in UNCLOS III.[72]

Marius Gjetnes's *Master's Thesis of Law* also assumes there are formations that qualify as Article 121(3) islands. He posits a concept not seen in other literature but is nonetheless logical. The UNLOS III convention regarded the regime of islands as a method to benefit the population thereof, and, therefore, even if a village was built on stilts on a low-tide elevation, the people of the village would have rights to an exclusive economic zone.

This concept was extracted by Gjetnes from the *Yearbook of the International Law Commission*, Vol. 1 (1954). The issue raised by this concept is which should come first, the stilt village or the exclusive economic

70 Brown quoting Imperial Conference 1923. Report of Inter-Departmental Committee on the Limits of Territorial Waters.
71 Barry Hart Dubner, "The Spratly 'Rocks' Dispute—a 'Rockapelago' Defies Norms of International Law," *Comparative Law Journal*, Temple University Beasley School of Law.
72 Joyner, 1999, 57.

zone (EEZ)? Gjetnes follows this line of reasoning by writing about 121(3) islands, and his conclusion is that if there is no indigenous population, an extended maritime zone should not be permitted under international law. In other words, the EEZ should come first—not the stilt village.

The People's Republic of China's position on whether uninhabited islands should generate exclusive economic zones varies with the situation. In the Spratlys, China has built artificial structures on low-tide elevations and presumably will claim the ocean area around the formation as theirs. On the other hand, when addressing the same issue concerning the waters near Okinotori Island, China takes an opposite position. Okinotori Island is uninhabited and only several meters high at low water, is slightly above sea level at high tide, and is formed by mere rocks. The Japanese are attempting to "grow" and expand the formation by seeding live coral on its fringes. By so doing, Japan is attempting to lay a foundation for claiming the formation as the basis for an exclusive economic zone, as it is "naturally formed." China argues that this rock does not warrant the establishment of an EEZ around it.[73]

The United Nations, Division for Ocean Affairs and the Law of the Sea, published an overview of UNCLOS III statements outlining the convention's work. It chose to emphasize Article 121(3) as a "key feature" of the convention with the following entry:

> The limits of the territorial sea, the exclusive economic zone and continental shelf of islands are determined in accordance with rules applicable to land territory, but rocks which could not sustain human habitation or economic life of their own would have no economic zone or continental shelf (UN, 2004).

The Division of Ocean Affairs chose this particular section from the entire convention to highlight; it follows then that Article 121(3) is more important than other sections, and one may assume with some certainty that the staff

---

73 Michelle Mark, "Amid Chinese Territory Dispute, Japan to Grow an Island out of Coral," *International Business Times,* December 26, 2015, accessed at http://www.ibtimes.com/amid-chinese-territory-disputes-japan-grow-island-out-coral-2240251 on January 14, 2016.

of the Division for Ocean Affairs and the Law of the Sea are for limiting the small ocean dots to only a territorial sea.

As a United States Naval officer, I navigated a 4,500-ton ship through the Spratlys and Paracels on aircraft search and rescue in 1965. Our transits were made during daylight and with extra watches posted in various visually advantageous positions on the ship. During extensive pattern sweeps through these formations, I did not leave the bridge, and I never noticed signs of any administrative control over the formations by anyone. Administrative control is one of the critical issues used by a nation in claiming sovereignty over a formation located in the open sea. China did nothing to interfere with our transit.

Rocks Versus Islands

As previously stated, all ocean formations remaining above the highest high-water tide line are considered "rocks" as defined in UNCLOS III (1982). This definition then includes shoals, reefs, sand bars, soil formations, and of course rocks. China is claiming all of these formations from her southern shores down to the fourth degree north latitude. And it continues to rattle sabers when any nation challenges its rights to control these formations and surrounding waters.

Assume if you will that China's rights as sovereign over all these formations is recognized by all nations and the United Nations. What does China actually have? Since none of these formations can sustain an economic life of their own or human habitation, China would be able to legally control waters from the shoreline of the formation out to twelve nautical miles (territorial waters). The drafters of UNCLOS III 1982 seemed to have been vague about defining what ocean formations qualified under the treaty to support an exclusive economic zone. Common sense and logic would dictate that very small, uninhabitable ocean formations should not generate large resource zones. Because of the vagueness of Article 121(3), China will surely argue it has a right to an EEZ for some, if not all, of the formations.

Legal precedent is of no help because no authoritative court or tribunal has ever provided a basis for *stare decisis* on this issue. The world came close to having a ruling when the International Court of Justice (ICJ) adjudicated the Black Sea case between Romania and Ukraine.[74] The arguments presented by each party were similar to what may be future arguments between China and one or more of the littoral nations of the South China Sea.

Romania argued Ukraine's rock, Serpent Island, could not sustain human habitation or economic life of its own because it lacked natural water sources and was devoid of soil, vegetation, and fauna. Romania also argued human survival on the rock was dependent on supplies consisting of water and food from off island. In reference to the alternate requirement of sustaining an economic life on its own, Romania argued there was nothing on the rock capable of supporting any form of economy. Romania's argument would probably be parroted by any of the claimants of South China Sea ocean formations.

Ukraine's argument commenced with the statement that the formation was "indisputably an island"—interesting, the word *indisputably* is currently used by China anytime it discusses sovereignty over formations in the sea. The argument consisted of statements that the formation did have sufficient vegetation and sufficient supply of fresh water. Ukraine continued arguing the formation had appropriate buildings and accommodation for an active population.

Today's reality is that the approximately one hundred persons consisting of frontier guard servicepersons and their families living on the formation are supplied water and supplies by air and sea. Unfortunately for the world, the ICJ decided it did not need to consider whether the formation falls under Article 121(2) or 121(3) to determine the maritime boundary. On the other hand, a former justice of the International Tribunal for the Law of the Sea, Judge Budislav Vukas of Croatia, provided the world with an idea of how Article 121(3) should be interpreted. His ideas were incorporated in the following statement:

10. The purpose of this brief text is to explain my belief that the establishment of exclusive economic zones around rocks and other small islands serves no useful purpose and that it is contrary to international law.

---

74 *Maritime Delimitation in the Black Sea (Romania v Ukraine)*, ICJ Rep 61, 2009.

It is interesting to note Ambassador Arvid Pardo—the main architect of the contemporary law of the sea—warned the international community of the danger of such a development back in 1971. In the United Nations Seabed Committee he stated this:

> If a 200 mile limit of jurisdiction could be founded on the possession of uninhabited, remote or very small islands, the effectiveness of international administration of ocean space beyond national jurisdiction would be gravely impaired.

The annexed map showing Australia's exclusive economic zone around Heard Island and the McDonald Islands, provided by the Agent of the Respondent, confirms that Ambassador Pardo's fear has been borne out.

Heard and McDonald islands are a volcanic formation of approximately eleven by thirteen nautical miles with very little flat land available for agriculture. The formation is generally covered in snow and would provide adequate water supply for inhabitants but not for sufficient agriculture to sustain a viable population. It is located at fifty-three degrees south latitude, with Mawson Peak at its center reaching 2,745 meters. Ambassador Pardo's fear was that nations claiming sovereignty over ocean rocks and then establishing EEZs of 400 nautical miles in diameter around these formations would create global problems of policing the rights of nations to natural resources found in the 126,500-square-nautical-mile area of ocean.

Rocks with Improvements

Putting together the previous definitions with the communist/socialist history of China, one can now understand China's logic and pattern of conquest of the South China Sea it has been following since its 1974 attack on Vietnam's Paracel Islands and every action it has taken since then to complete the assimilation of the South China Sea and, perhaps in the future, the domination of the littoral nations bordering the sea.

The best friend the Chinese have is UNCLOS III 1982 and its Article 121. It vagueness and inability to provide the world with a precise definition of what ocean formations rate an EEZ allows all nations to argue as they please to claim such a zone. A very simple addition to Article 121 was already codified in a Resolution of the Imperial Conference 1923 laying out a common policy for the British Empire to follow. For example, the following excerpts from the resolutions would have helped the world settle these issues:

The coastline from the low-water mark of which the 3-mile limit of territorial waters should be measured, is that of the mainland and also that of all islands. The word "island" covers all portions of territory permanently above high water in normal circumstances and capable of use or habitation.[75]

The conference members also provided a memorandum helping define the terms used:

22. The phrase "capable of use or habitation" has been adopted as a compromise. It is intended that the words "capable of use" should mean, capable, without artificial addition, of being used throughout all seasons for some definite commercial or defense purpose, and that "capable of habitation" should mean capable, without artificial addition, of permanent human habitation.

23. It is recognized that these criteria will in many cases admit of argument, but nothing more definite could be arrived at in view of the many divergent considerations involved. It is thought that no criteria could be selected that would not be open to some form of criticism.[76]

---

75 Imperial Conference 1923. Report of Inter-Departmental Committee on the Limits of Territorial Waters (Document T.118/118/380, 1924); Public Record Office Ref. F.O. 372/2108, 5.
76 Ibid.

This simple addition would have eased the burden of the South China Sea formation claimants fending off the Chinese but would not have provided sufficient legal basis for a clean defeat and thwarting of China's desire to be the center of the world.

Today it is easy to predict China's next move in the South China Sea. Now that the enlargement of the formations using artificial means allows for airfields, missile batteries, and territorial seas around these man-made formations, China will probably allow the hostilities to cool off but never back down from its claims to the entire sea.

After a suitable period for the world's attention to be diverted to other conflicts and for the United States to get another administration that decimates our national defense forces and continues to appease aggressors, China will then start claiming its man-made formations are *islands* as the term is used in Article 121(3) of UNCLOS III and start treating the entire South China Sea as its exclusive economic zone. It is also probable that China may be so bold, based on its success since its 1974 hostile take-over of the Paracels, to claim the entire sea as its territorial waters and deny safe passage to all ships and aircraft on, over, and under its waters.

CHAPTER 5

How the South China Sea's Littoral Nations and the World Lost Its Freedom of Navigation of This Sea

CHARLES LIU, WRITING FOR THE *Loyola of Los Angeles International & Comparative Law Journal* in 1996, had a different opinion from the mainstream non-Beijing-dominated sources. His paper will be used to highlight these differences to provide the reader with dissenting opinions.

Liu's position that Brunei declared sovereignty over the Spratlys is incorrect and probably just an oversight, but the position the claimants will negotiate under international law was erroneous and based on a self-serving statement made by Beijing. Liu mistakenly interpreted a statement made by then Foreign Minister Qian Qichen at the ASEAN meeting in July 1995 as a change in China's policy.

A typical misunderstanding of UNCLOS III was highlighted by Liu's statement: "By virtue of the exclusive economic zones granted under UNCLOS, sovereignty over the Spratlys nets exclusive control over its surrounding resources." His supporting footnote only explained that "islands" may have an EEZ. The problem was defining which of the formations are islands, if any are. Another point of contention was characterized by Liu's position that "sovereignty over the Spratlys will yield impressive natural resource wealth." The issue is not the wealth, but rather the assumption that sovereignty must be over all the Spratlys.[77]

---

77 Charles Liu, "Chinese Sovereignty and Joint Development: A Pragmatic Solution to the Spratly Islands Dispute," 18 Loy. *L.A. Int'l & Comp. L.J.* 865, 1996.

Whoever gains sovereignty over the South China Sea formations would gain significant influence over international shipping. Liu's premise is possibly based on the Japanese using Itu Aba as a submarine base during World War II and China's 1992 territorial sea law requiring warships to obtain permission before transiting most of the South China Sea.[78] Specifically Article 6 of China's Law on the Territorial Sea and the Contiguous Zone of 25 February 1992 reads: "To enter the territorial sea of the People's Republic of China, foreign military ships must obtain permission from the Government of the People's Republic of China."

This restriction on peaceful transit of other nations' warships contradicts the term of UNCLOS III to which China is a signatory. Article 38 of the convention reads as follows:

Article38
Right of transit passage

1. In straits referred to in article 37, all ships and aircraft enjoy the right of transit passage, which shall not be impeded; except that, if the strait is formed by an island of a State bordering the strait and its mainland, transit passage shall not apply if there exists seaward of the island a route through the high seas or through an exclusive economic zone of similar convenience with respect to navigational and hydrographical characteristics.

2. Transit passage means the exercise in accordance with this Part of the freedom of navigation and overflight solely for the purpose of continuous and expeditious transit of the strait between one part of the high seas or an exclusive economic zone and another part of the high seas or an exclusive economic zone. However, the requirement of continuous and expeditious transit does not preclude passage through the strait for the purpose of entering, leaving or returning from a State

---

78 Ibid.

bordering the strait, subject to the conditions of entry to that State.

3. Any activity which is not an exercise of the right of transit passage through a strait remains subject to the other applicable provisions of this Convention.

No distinction is made between nonwarships and warships. The United States Department of Defense reiterated the settled position in International Maritime Law (1992) using the following words: "One of the fundamental tenets in the international law of the sea is the right enjoyed by all ships of every nation to innocent passage through another state's territorial sea."[79]

Liu and others have raised alarm over control of the shipping lanes; is this a real threat, and should other states be alarmed? The submarine issue has been overtaken by events. Submarines can now patrol the entire world and be based anywhere. In reference to the 1992 Chinese legislation, China has not filed a baseline for any of the formations in the Spratlys, and as discussed here, the baseline for the Paracels violates major provisions of UNCLOS III. Should any sovereign interfere with shipping and the sea lines of communication, hopefully the United Nations would take action against the offending state before the offended state retaliated with force.

When the Paracel Islands were invaded by China, and Vietnam attempted to defend its territory, the United States refused to assist Vietnam in doing so. The United States and the Republic of South Vietnam were both signatories and members of the Southeast Asia Treaty Organization (SEATO). The American giant was in the process of licking its wounds suffered while attempting to support South Vietnam against the combined forces of Russia, China, and North Vietnam in accordance with the terms of the above-mentioned treaty. As a result of the giant's inaction, the Chinese learned that there are times when the American giant chooses to ignore its treaty obligations based on internal political problems.

---

79 US Department of State, Bureau of Oceans and International Environmental and Scientific Affairs, "United States Responses to Excessive National Maritime Claims," *Limits in the Seas*, No. 112, March 9, 1992, 51, accessed at http://www.state.gov/documents/organization/58381.pdf on June 16, 2007.

It is important to remember that South Vietnam requested the US Seventh Fleet help defend its islands, and the United States refused to come to their aid. As noted, the Vietnamese protested the belligerent and aggressive behavior of the Chinese to the United Nations; however, their efforts were blocked by China using its veto power.[80] The American sleeping giant did nothing to help its ally.

This warlike stance taken by the Chinese has continued to this day, and China continues to use its veto power in the United Nations to force the world into accepting communism and socialism as the only acceptable method of governing. One of the problems dealing with the rhetoric of the Chinese is how they use the definitions of various waters of the oceans—reading five years of news and rhetoric produced by China confirmed that their use of terms designating areas of the world's oceans does not, at times, conform to the official definitions as noted in the United Nations Law of the Sea Treaty.

Another tactic used by China to extend its control and quasi sovereignty over disputed rocks and islets located in the EEZ of another country is to file false (nonconforming) baselines with the United Nations. By so doing, the Chinese government probably knows there will be opposition, but since the UN does not do anything about these bogus filings, China just sits back and waits for the objections to wane.

For example, on September 24, 2012, China filed new coordinates of straight baselines in the East China Sea. These new baselines enclose two groups of formations claimed by China, Japan, and Taiwan (called Senkaku by Japan, Diaoyu by China, Tiaoyutai by Taiwan, and Pinnacle by Great Britain). Japan immediately protested the filing, and the United Nations and the United States (under the Obama administration) did nothing. The United Nations has done nothing to enforce the terms of UNCLOS III concerning baseline coordinates.

Customary international law and UNCLOS III have delineated specific requirements for nations to draw baselines based on two separate concepts.

---

80 On October 25, 1971, the majority of members of the United Nations voted to oust the Republic of China and admit the People's Republic of China, giving a permanent member seat to another communist nation. By so doing, the majority of the General Assembly voted to support the proposition that the takeover of China by an armed force with aggression led by Mao Tse-tung was a legitimate transfer of power. This act of the United Nations spat in the face of international law and recognized force as a method of acquiring territory or changing a government.

The first is using the coastline of the mainland of the nation, and the second is as a method for determining baselines for archipelagic states such as the Philippines. For mainland coastal baselines, the accepted international law is based on Article 4(1) of the Geneva Convention and Section 2, Article 7(1) of the UNCLOS III Convention, with both reading as follows:

1. In localities where the coastline is deeply indented and cut into, or if there is a fringe of islands along the coast in its immediate vicinity, the method of straight baselines joining appropriate points may be employed in drawing the baseline from which the breadth of the territorial sea is measured.[81, 82]

For archipelagic states, UNCLOS III, Part IV, Article 47 provides nine specifications for drawing baselines as discussed as follows concerning the Paracel Islands (reefs). The basis for using these techniques for drawing baselines is that the state must be an "archipelagic" state. China does not meet the requirements for such a classification. Article 46 provides the following definitions:

(a) "archipelagic State" means a State constituted wholly by one or more archipelagos and may include other islands;
(b) "archipelagos" means a group of islands, including parts of islands, interconnecting waters and other natural features which are so closely interrelated that such islands, waters and other natural features form an intrinsic geographical, economic and political entity, or which historically have been regarded as such.

By not meeting the requirements of being an archipelagic state, China must conform to the straight baselines as defined by customary international law and UNCLOS III. The coordinates submitted should be rejected by the United Nations based on two lines of reasoning. The first is that China,

---

81 1958 Geneva Conventions of the Law of the Sea, Geneva, April 29, 1958.
82 United Nations Convention on the Law of the Sea of December 10, 1982.

contrary to its self-proclamation, is not the undisputed sovereign of Huangwei Yu, Bei Yu, Nan Yu, Diaoyu Dao, Fei Yu, Bei Xiaodao, Nan Xiaodao, or ChiweiYu, which are the formations enclosed within the coordinates submitted. This is not the first time China has attempted to gain recognition of sovereignty by drawing a map and then declaring sovereignty. The use of the Nine-Ten-Eleven-Dashed (Dot) Line Maps was the first example used by China followed by the Paracel Islands baseline filing.

China has at least a forty-four-year history of patiently pushing for more and more control of the South China Sea, and it has accomplished its goals at the expense of the littoral nations and the world. The nations bordering the sea do not have the military capacity of China and cannot possibly defeat it in a pitched battle over the formations. China refuses to arbitrate and allow any international tribunal to adjudicate any issue involving the sovereignty of the formations. There were lulls in China's attention to its expansion goals in the sea for extended periods of time when China was occupied elsewhere, such as her Indian and Vietnamese incursions. And it is important to note that even when China's leaders were courting President Nixon and Secretary Kissinger, the country attacked Vietnam and allied itself with the Khmer Rouge and Pol Pot.

If there is one word to describe how China has been so successful since 1974 in forcing the world out of the South China Sea, it would be *appeasement*. The littoral nations had little or no choice because they could not stand up to China economically or militarily without a strong ally such as the United States. But the United States was not willing to stand against China at any time since we lost to the Vietnamese, Russian, and Chinese forces and abandoned the military support promised to South Vietnam through our joining the South East Asia Treaty Organization (SEATO).

In Korea our forces were not allowed to attack the real military forces we faced in Korea—Russia and China. In Vietnam our forces were not allowed, once again, to attack Russian ships supplying weapons and supplies to SEATO's communist enemies. Nowhere did the US government take a strong stance against China and Russia such as embargos designed to financially cripple these countries. True, our leaders were afraid of another world war, but appeasement does nothing but delay war or, in the alternative, domination by the belligerence of the appeaser.

The United States declared to the world it was not recognizing China's sovereignty over formations by sending aircraft and ships to the vicinity of those formations. It appears Obama's secretaries of state failed to advise the president that when a United States–flagged ship skirts one of the Chinese-held formations and stays outside the twelve-nautical-mile territorial sea, the United States is recognizing and confirming the sovereignty of China over that rock. Additionally, the United States has a right to peacefully transit the territorial water of another state without notice—notwithstanding China's attempt to limit that right by its 1992 act previously documented. The United States has no such act—it complies with the terms of UNCLOS III.

CHAPTER 6

Philippines Versus People's Republic of China Arbitration

———

THE PHILIPPINES ARE THE FIRST littoral nation of the South China Sea to obtain a hearing on a sovereignty issue of a formation close to its coastline. As of this writing, the Chinese government has already taken the position it will not abide by any decision made by the distinguished arbitral panel. One issue that may be addressed by the panel is the definition of an island as used in Article 121(3) of UNCLOS. It will probably not be decided because the formations that are the subject of the arbitration are merely rocks, and it is obvious they cannot support human habitation or an economic life of their own.

THE NINE-TEN-ELEVEN-DASHED (DOTS) LINE MAP

The current government of the People's Republic of China does not address the issue as to what prompted the Kuomintang (KMT) to form the Land and Water Maps Inspection Committee to take on the task of defining the KMT's maritime domain to the south of its territory. When you review the news releases and statements made by the current Chinese government, you will not find any reference to the KMT's map revision committee. To understand what prompted the KMT government to form such a committee for the purposes of revising the maritime domain of China, it is important to review what was going on in China in 1933.

Should the Obama administration actually exercise our rights to help our Asian allies and exercise the terms of the United Nations Law of the Sea III and force China to back down using military force, China will either fight the United States and its allies or continue to claim it has the right to do what it wants in the South China Sea. A possible starting point for China's argument, should it chose not to fight, would be using its historic claim to the sea. The president of the United States, be it Obama or his successor, should exercise our rights with confidence that China has been violating the terms of UNCLOS III and the previous versions of the Law of the Sea since 1974.

China has and always will use time and the instability of American foreign policy to beat the free world into submission. Its current claim to the South China Sea, all its formations, and surrounding waters started in the 1930s.

On June 7, 1933, the Chinese government formed the Land and Water Maps Inspection Committee for the purpose of revising China's maps and to define its maritime domain of the South China Sea. In April of the same year, the committee proclaimed that China held sovereignty over all the South China Sea down to the fourth degree north latitude. In April of 1935, the committee issued a map delineating the entire South China Sea as its possession and its "living places of Chinese fishermen."

In releasing a Chinese map with ten dashes (dots) outlining its alleged sovereignty area of the South China Sea, China claimed the Natuna Island group in which Indonesia now has natural gas wells, the Philippines' Malampaya and Camago natural gas and condensate fields, Malaysia's natural gas fields located off the shore of Sarawak, and many Vietnamese oil fields. The fishing rights for the entire South China Sea were also claimed by the Chiang Kai-shek–led Kuomintang (KMT) government. No nation objected to the Chinese claims to the South China Sea because the ten-dashed maps were not published until decades after they were first drawn.

REASONS FOR FORMING THE LAND AND WATER MAPS INSPECTION COMMITTEE

One must understand the Chinese ability to remove "time" as a factor from any decision made by its leadership. Americans and Westerners in general tend to place a time dimension on any decision-making process, including negotiating with other parties. The time dimension then becomes an irrelevant factor placing an artificial restraint on completion of any decision-making process or achieving a desired result. When reviewing Chinese leadership's past decisions and negotiations, it becomes obvious that the time dimension for reaching conclusions is missing. The delayed use of the maps produced by the Land and Water Maps Inspection Committee is a prime example.

In history the period between 1927 and 1937 is generally referred to as the Nanjing Decade. At the start of this period, the nationalist government did not have control of Manchuria nor was it able to control the warlords that dominated many parts of the country. The KMT was dealing with the economic impact of the world's financial depression of 1929, the Japanese invasion of Manchuria on the east coast of China, the warlords' large armies, and the political pressure exerted by Russia supporting Mao Tse-tung.

Additionally, the KMT only controlled 8 percent of the geographical area and 25 percent of the population and was having difficulty collecting taxes to support the Nanjing government. The Chinese people were also becoming leery of the KMT's monopoly of military and political power, and on top of these problems, many objected to the KMT's policy of appeasing foreigners and its failure to counter increased Japanese aggression in Manchuria. Funds and manpower were also being expended by the newly formed KMT in attempting to overcome the communist threat backed by Russia.

In the beginning of the Japanese occupation of Manchuria, the Kwantung Army a group of the Imperial Japanese Army supported them. The Japanese considered Manchuria as theirs because tens of thousands of Japanese troops died in the area during the 1904–1905 Russo-Japanese War. KMT leadership also believed that the Japanese in control of Manchuria would provide a geographical barrier between the area of China controlled by the KMT and Russia.

This amicable arrangement between the KMT and Japan existed up until January 1932, when the Japanese invaded Shanghai to avert attention from their Manchurian conquests. The KMT was forced to retreat to the Luoyang in central China and requested international support. International mediation led by the United Kingdom of Great Britain and Northern Ireland using the League of Nations as its tool was successful in forcing the Japanese to evacuate Shanghai in May 1932.

One must consider why the Japanese gave up Shanghai; the only logical reason would be fear of waging war against Great Britain—the main proponent of the May 1932 armistice, which established a protected zone around Shanghai and lifted the embargo. The United States at this moment in history had no effect on the armistice because of political isolationism and the lack of an effective military. We as a nation must stand up to China and regain our military position in the world; the importance of doing this can be supported by Japan's action to abandon Shanghai in May of 1932. At that time, the United States was isolationist and chose not to participate in world affairs. On the other hand, Great Britain dominated the world's oceans. Great Britain was the prime mover in preparing and negotiating the armistice treaty requiring Japan to leave Shanghai and the development of a protected zone around the city to allow trade and commerce to resume. Japan agreed to the terms of the armistice and left Shanghai because of the military power of Great Britain and its lease of Hong Kong, BCC. However, the Japanese still controlled the eastern seaboard of China.

With the Japanese in control of the eastern seaboard of China, it seems logical that the KMT would look to the South China Sea for a future source of food to replace its control of the eastern coast of the mainland.

Apparently there are no documents accessible to Western research concerning the formation of the map revision committee, but it seems logical that to ensure the growth and stability of the KMT-controlled southern area of China, it would be necessary to have control and dominion of the sea south of the mainland. And since the Eleven-Dashed-Line Map was not published to anyone outside of China until many years later, one can only speculate as to the true intention of the Chinese nationalist government. It also seems logical that because of Japan's invasion of China in 1937 and the continual pressure from communist organizations to set up a joint government with the KMT, the newly drawn map with the eleven dashes was probably forgotten and set aside. There was no rest for the Chinese until after the victory over Japan and Germany.[83]

INITIAL USE OF THE DASHED (DOTS) MAP

Immediately after cessation of hostilities in World War II, the world and the US giant went back to sleep after having been awakened by the Japanese attack on Pearl Harbor and the German blitzkrieg of Poland. Dr. Zheng Wang, the director of the Center for Peace and Conflict Studies at Seton Hall University, alleges that while the giant slept and healed its wounds an eighth-grade geography textbook published by the People's Education Press in 1947 used the Nine-Dashed-Line Map as a learning tool for students to measure the distance between the most southern area of the South China Sea claimed by China to its coastline.[84]

I have not been able to confirm Dr. Wang's statement; however, I believe it is true, and he must possess one of the textbooks. The reasons why I believe his statement is that during my five years teaching in China, I found that university students had learned many facts that were not true concerning geopolitics as related to the People's Republic of China. In his short article on the subject, Dr. Wang discussed the 1933 Eleven-Dashed (Dot) Map and the 1936 Bai Meichu map.

While I believe it is true that the Nine-Dashed-Line Map was engraved in the hearts of Chinese students, I do not believe that provides any admissible

---

83 *Modern Chinese History III: The Nanjing Decade 1927–1937*, accessed at www.chinafolio. com/modern-chinese-history-1937-1937 on October 24, 2009. I am grateful to ChinaFolio for preparing an excellent recap of information I had previously studied while in China—their work made mine more efficient.

84 Dr. Wang noted that the original map was an Eleven-Dashed (Dot) Line version and Zhou En-lai had two dashes (dots) removed in the Gulf of Tonkin prior to publication in the textbook for the eighth grade. See footnote immediately following.

evidence that could be submitted to an unbiased international tribunal concerning the validity of claims to the South China Sea. A legal issue is generated as to when the map was first published for review by other nations of the world and not when the People's Republic of China started indoctrinating students using lies about the extent of sovereignty over open seas.[85]

It is important to understand the original Eleven-Dashed-Line Map was published by the KMT Government of the Republic of China, December 1947. Zhou En-lai reduced the number of dashes from eleven to nine, and this version of the map has continued as one of the bases for China claiming Taiwan and Spratly and Paracel islands.[86] The publication of the Nine-Dashed-Line Map shortly after Mao came to power on October 1, 1949, is consistent with the Communist Party's agenda to think in terms of accomplishing their goals using generations as a time line rather than the Western way of using political terms in office as a basis for establishing geopolitical norms.

By indoctrinating young students early, it would be easier to have these future adults supporting the idea that the South China Sea was national waters. The critical word is *publication* and whether or not the Nine-Dashed-Line Map was published in such a fashion to allow other nations to object to the map. Dr. Wang did not provide specific dates for the initial publication of the textbook, but it must have been shortly after October 1, 1949, when the People's Republic of China was formed with Mao Tse-tung as president and Zhou En-lai as premier.

China has not continued to push the map as if it had some magical properties that would allow it to take control of the entire South China Sea. But in 2002 China issued new passports that included the Nine-Dashed-Line Map on the insert, probably as an attempt to argue in the future that when other countries allowed Chinese citizens carrying this new passport to enter, they

---

85 "The Nine-Dashed Line: 'Engraved in Our Hearts,'" 2014, accessed at http://the diplomat.com/2014/08/the-nine-dashed-line-engraved-in-our-hearts. Dr. Zheng Wang is the director of the Center for Peace and Conflict Studies, Seton Hall University, and a global fellow at the Woodrow Wilson Center.

86 Peter J. Brown, "Calculated Ambiguity in the South China Sea," *Asia Times Online*, December 8, 2009, accessed February 5, 2014.

would be acknowledging China's right to control the area of the South China Sea enclosed by the nine dashes.

President Clinton and Secretary of State Albright did nothing to thwart China's attempt to propagandize the world with its false theory of the value of the map. The State Department did issue a statement (Victoria Nuland spokeswoman) that said the United States had concerns about China's map causing "tension and anxiety" between countries in the South China Sea. Notice the carefully worded statement does not address whether or not President Clinton or Secretary Albright had any concerns.

The Philippines, on the other hand, immediately stopped visa stamping Chinese passports containing the map so as not to allow China the political position that by stamping such passports the Philippines recognized China's sovereignty over the South China Sea.

The charade continued in June 2014 when China once again modified the map to include more area enclosed by ten dashes. In this version of the map, China included territories disputed with India. President Obama and Secretary Kerry did nothing to counter the change either publicly or through our ambassador to the United Nations.

One final modification made to the map of China was changing from using a description box in the bottom right-hand corner to an elongated version where the Chinese mainland and the disputed area of the South China Sea are included on one map. During all these changes and modifications, the US leaders continued to ignore the Chinese farce of claiming territory merely by including it on a map. International law has never recognized a nation's territorial expansion merely by issuing a new map.

If this practice was acceptable under international law, the new world would still be divided based on the terms of the Treaty of Tordesillas between Spain and Portugal. This treaty was signed and ratified by Spain and Portugal in 1494 and divided the world into two major dominions. The Treaty of Tordesillas did have an effect on the development of many nations but ultimately was discarded and ignored.

If the Chinese argue historic maps decide the fate of territories and oceans, then Spain and Portugal would have legal claims to the Americas and Canada.

Continuing this line of reasoning, Japan would have claims over large areas of China by claiming sovereignty over the territories it controlled in the past. Even Mongolia would have claims to northern parts of China they invaded and occupied in the thirteenth century.

The American giant, during all the map modifications and subsequent Chinese claims, has continued to ignore China's effort to dominate and control the open seas over which half the world's ships transit. Occasionally words are uttered by our leaders and are promptly ignored or ridiculed by the Chinese. The giant did open an eyelid and with a very passive whisper made some statements concerning the Nine-Dashed-Line Map.

Ambassador Jeffrey A. Bader was very kind and diplomatic when he described the position of the giant as stated by Assistant Secretary of State for East Asian and Pacific Affairs Danny Russell before the House Committee on Foreign Affairs on February 5, 2014, paraphrased as follows: Any claim to maritime rights based on the publication of a map would not be consistent with international law, and maritime rights must be based on land features.

Assistant Secretary Russell, in my opinion, weakened his clarification of the US position by continuing with the following: "The international community would welcome China to clarify or adjust its Nine-Line claim to bring it in accordance with the International Law of the Sea."[87]

Surely the Chinese interpreted Secretary Russell's final comments granting them the right to "adjust" the Nine-Line Map, so somehow it would become acceptable under the terms of the United Nations Law of the Sea, 1982 (UNCLOS III). The only way to accomplish this feat would be to file proper baselines with the United Nations for any land formation it claims. Once the baselines were properly identified and published, then the littoral nations of the South China Sea could place their case before the General Assembly and the United Nations and argue before appointed tribunals any sovereignty issues.

---

87 Jeffrey A. Bader, "The U.S. and China's Nine-Dash Line: Ending the Ambiguity," 2014, accessed at http://www.brookings.edu/research/opinions/2014/02/06-us-china-nine-dash-line-bader.

CHINA'S POLITICAL USE OF THE DASHED (DOTS) MAP

The PRC's position on how they intend to argue before the world the significance of the current Ten-Dashed-Line Map is not clear. What is clear can be identified by their actions and not their words. In reference to words, it appears the People's Republic of China, surely at the direction of the Chinese Communist Party, instructed everyone discussing the South China Sea to use the following phrase: "China's sovereignty over the Huangyan Island is indisputable."[88]

This phrase appears in almost all literature and speeches related to the South China Sea disputes written or made by Chinese government representatives. The only thing that changes is the name of the target feature.

Huangyan Island has been listed on the International Chart Series as Scarborough Reef since it was first published.[89] The People's Republic of China never filed a complaint with the United Kingdom for using the name "Scarborough Reef." China has always been quick to note the slightest questioning of their "indisputable sovereignty" by other nations, but it has ignored the world's most reputable chart makers—the United Kingdom.

The Chinese consistently refer to Scarborough Reef as an island in the latest round of confrontation, which was started by them in 2009 with the Philippines. The Obama administration did not object or even take notice of the subtle use of the word *island* or its implication. This appears to be done to support a future claim to a four-hundred-nautical-mile-diameter exclusive economic zone based on the United Nation's Law of the Sea (UNCLOS III) requiring an "island" be a required land feature for such a claim. One of the requirements for a formation to qualify as an island is that it be capable of supporting an economic life of its own or human life as previously detailed.[90]

---

88 See example at *China's Sovereignty over the Huangyan Island Is Indisputable*, Philippine's Chinese Embassy (May 27, 2012) accessed at http://ph.china-embassy.org/eng/xwfb/t935925. htm on February 5, 2014.

89 Hydrographic Chart Number 3489; South China Sea—Northeast Part; Manila to Hong Kong; published at Tauton, United Kingdom, May 28, 1998, under the Superintendence of Rear J. P. Clark, CB, LBO, MBE, Hydrographer for the navy; chart contains updated Notices to Mariners through 2005.

90 UNCLOS III, Regime of Islands, Article 121, 3: "Rocks which cannot sustain human habitation or economic life of their own shall have no exclusive economic zone or Continental shelf."

Figure 4. Scarborough Reef with Stele

The Chinese insist that the rock depicted in the photo can sustain human habitation or an economic life of its own. True there are other small rocks that form a circle and act as a reef around a central lagoon, but none of them are connected, and they are difficult to approach during heavy weather. The events surrounding Scarborough Reef and its occupation by the Chinese and subsequent Chinese publicity may be used as a model for all past, similar actions and possibly even for future Chinese encroachment on formations in the South China Sea claimed and even occupied by other nations.

An article published by *The Diplomat* on November 1, 2012, provides an excellent synopsis of an apparent change in tactics by the PRC as related to the formations found in the South China Sea.[91] Scarborough Shoal (Reef) prior to April 2012 was used by fishermen from the Philippines, Vietnam, Taiwan, and China without incident. The circular reef measures approximately eight

---

91   China's Island Strategy, "Redefine the Status Quo," accessed at http://thediplomat.com/2012/11/chinas-island-strategy-redefine-the-status-quo/ on February 20 2014.

nautical miles across at its widest point and consists of nothing more than rocks—some of which are exposed only at low tide. Neither the Filipinos nor the Chinese maintained any presence on these rocks, the largest of which is depicted in the picture.

For approximately thirty years, the Philippines arrested Chinese fishermen who were inside the shoal. The PRC mounted no military efforts to control these rock formations until April 2012. To be fair, the People's Republic of China did protest when the Republic of the Philippines filed its baseline with the United Nations in May 2009.[92] The initial action consisted of several Chinese ships blocking the entrance to the shoal to prevent the arrest of its country's fishermen. After the Chinese fishermen left the shoal area, both Filipino and Chinese vessels remained in the area. By the end of May, China had deployed up to seven ships in the vicinity of Scarborough Shoal.

Apparently the Chinese and Filipino governments agreed to withdraw their ships; this information was originally only made public in the Philippines. Disregarding the agreement, Chinese ships returned to patrol the area, and they roped off the only entrance to the lagoon enclosed by the circle of rocks outlining the reef to control access by the Philippines.[93]

Shortly after the Chinese ships commenced controlling Scarborough Shoal, an extensive article was published in the *People's Daily* on May 10, 2012, itemizing five reasons why China had a legal basis for sovereignty over this formation of rocks inside the EEZ of the Philippine Republic. The reasons consisted of the following points:

1. China was the first country to discover and exercise jurisdiction over this formation.
2. China had been developing and utilizing the rock formation since 1977.
3. The Philippines have no right to claim sovereignty over the shoal.

---

92 Mia M. Gonzalez and Estrella Torres, "Baselines Bill Signed; China Protests," *Top News*, accessed at http://businessmirror.com.ph/home/top-news/7365-baselines-bill-signed-china-protests.
93 China's Island Strategy.

4. The use of the rock formation by the United States and the Filipino governments as a target range was illegal.
5. The fact that Scarborough Shoal is closer to the Philippines than China is not a basis for claiming sovereignty.

The five points may be grouped as follows: 1, 3, and 4 are nothing more than conclusions of the Chinese leadership and would never serve as evidence before any tribunal without support and convincing arguments. The "developing and utilizing" consist of one stele placed on one of the rocks; no other use of the reef has been recorded. Number 5 completely misstates the facts: Scarborough Reef is within the EEZ claimed by the Philippines.

The only issue that will be addressed in this section is number 1 because it directly relates to the Ten-Dashed-Line Map.[94] The writer of the article lays out the history of the Dashed-Line Map in a statement that China published these maps in October 1947, changing the name to "Minzhu Reef." Readers should note once more that the Chinese did not publish this change by filing it with the United Nations nor notifying such dominant map makers of the world as the United Kingdom of Great Britain, the United States, or the Hydrographic Office of Brazil.

A second Chinese committee changed the name back to Huangyan Island and listed it as Chinese territory in 1983. No objection was raised by the Philippines or the US ambassador to the United Nations. One must disregard the rhetoric provided by the Chinese and attend to their acts of domination of all the area of the South China Sea enclosed within the Ten-Dashed-Line Map currently in vogue. If the Chinese logic and theory are reality, what about the claims of other littoral nations such as Vietnam and the Philippines?

Take for example the Vietnamese historical claims using the same concept. Vietnam can produce maps for examination by any arbiter that go back to the 1500s—the Asia map drawn by Gerard Mercator (1512–1594), the East India map by Pieter and Petrus in 1594, and the beautifully preserved maps of

---

94 "China Has Legal Basis for Sovereignty over Huangyan Island," *The People's Daily*, May 10, 2012, accessed at www.china.org.cn/opinion/2012-5/10/content_25348875.htm on May 12, 2012.

W. Blaeu (1645) and Visscher (1680), plus up to two hundred maps identified and cataloged by the Institute of Socio-Economic Research and Development Studies of Da Nang collected by Tran Thang.[95] All of these ancient maps drawn by persons of many different nations confirm Vietnam's claim using only historical maps as the basis for their claims.

The Republic of the Philippines approached the map issue from a different angle. In September 2014, the Philippines put on display over a hundred ancient maps dating back to the Song Dynasty (960 CE) and the Chiang Dynasty from the early twentieth century. This collection of ancient maps showed China only claiming as its southernmost territory Hainan Island just off the Chinese coast.[96]

China, notwithstanding the production of these ancient maps by the Philippines and Vietnam, which have as much credibility as its own, continues to point to the Ten-Dashed-Line Map as a source document supporting its claim to the entire South China Sea. China's claim based on historical maps should lose without question if placed before an impartial tribunal.

China's current reclamation and its construction of bases in the South China Sea provide them the equivalent of America's aircraft carriers as strategic bases for its military. References to the ancient maps seem to be taking a backseat to China's aggressive building projects—the littoral nations on the sea and their ally, the United States, have done nothing to stop China's illegal destruction of the formations claimed by multiple nations. The American giant, guided by the Obama administration, continues to issue only occasional grunts without taking any effective action.

---

95 Anh Son and Tra Xanh, no date, *Vietnam's Case for Sovereignty in the East Sea? An Abundance of History,* accessed at http://english.vietnamnet.vn/fms/special-reports/103752/vietnam-s-case-for-sovereignty-in-the-east-sea--an-abundance-of-history.html on May 12, 2014.

96 Manual Mogato, "Philippines Displays Ancient Maps to Debunk China's Sea Claims," 2014, accessed at reuters.com/article/2014/09/11/us-southchinasea-philippines-idUSKBN0H20140911 on May 12, 2014.

CHAPTER 7

China Will Only Negotiate With Individual Nations On South China Sea Issues

———

CHINA CONTINUALLY REFUSES TO SUBMIT its sovereignty disputes over the South China Sea formations to any world-respected adjudication tribunal or court. As noted before, China has announced to the world that it will not comply with any decision made by the arbitral tribunal in the Philippine versus China dispute over the sovereignty of several formations in the South China Sea. This accomplishment is more noteworthy because UNCLOS III specifically requires both litigants to approve litigation of issues involving the treaty.

The strategic move by the Philippines was not to attack the sovereignty issue directly but phrase its complaint as a maritime delimitation/entitlements issue. By so doing, the Philippines used Article 287 and Annex VII of UNCLOS to force an unwilling China to an adjudication of the issues. China, Russia, and their political allies have always blocked any treaty from containing words that would allow any nation to bring another nation before any court of justice unless both parties agreed to the adjudication. Naturally China always refuses to so agree when it feels it will lose.

In place of adjudicating the issues as civilized nations are wont to do, China prefers to force the small, defenseless littoral nations bordering the South China Sea into bilateral negotiations. Yet China continually announces it will never negotiate the sovereignty issue of any formation; China's position entails only negotiating some of the distribution of some of the assets of the formation in question. In past negotiations China brings large sums of money to the negotiating table with promises of peaceful coexistence, with the smaller nation taking the money and not disagreeing with China's policies anymore.

China's advantage is its skill at removing time as an issue; it is willing to wait a century if necessary to accomplish its goal. In contrast the US negotiators want results before the next election cycle, and small nations just want peace and an increase in national wealth.

CHINA'S AIR DEFENSE IDENTIFICATION ZONE EXPANSION

In late 2013, China unilaterally expanded its Air Defense Identification Zone (ADIZ). By so doing, it was requiring civilian aircraft transiting the ADIZ to have received prior permission from the Federal Aviation Administration (FAA), generally done by the Pilot in Command (PIC) filing a flight plan. When civilian (nonmilitary) aircraft enter an ADIZ without being identified, the aircraft will be subject to intercept by the ADIZ-protected country and, if necessary, attacked. The United States Department of Defense, in a statement signed by Christine E. Wormuth, Under Secretary of Defense for Policy, stated very clearly the internationally accepted procedures of delineating and transiting a foreign ADIZ. It reads as follows:

(1) Air Defense Identification Zones (ADIZs)

    a. DoD respects that a State may establish an ADIZ that geographically extends into the international airspace adjacent to the State's national airspace, but such ADIZs may not impede the rights, freedoms, and lawful uses of airspace under international law of foreign aircraft, including foreign military aircraft. An ADIZ provides a practical method for a State to identify aircraft as potential threats to the State's national security.

    b. DoD respects that other States may establish conditions for foreign aircraft to enter into their national airspace and airports, including adherence to reasonable ADIZ procedures. However,

> DoD does not recognize efforts by other States to impose such ADIZ procedures upon foreign aircraft that are only transiting international airspace within the State's ADIZ without any intention to enter the State's national airspace.
>
> c. DoD understands that a State's establishment of an ADIZ neither imputes any additional rights to that State that it does not otherwise enjoy under international law, nor does it expand any of those rights for that State. Thus, DoD understands that other States continue to enjoy, quantitatively and qualitatively, the same rights, freedoms, and lawful uses of the airspace reflected in international law that they did absent a State's establishment of an ADIZ.

The United States recognizes China's right to establish an ADIZ but does not recognize any restrictions of those rights of any aircraft to transit an ADIZ that is not only transiting international airspace within China's ADIZ. What China did in expanding its ADIZ was to include international airspace. International airspace is considered the space immediately above open oceans and seas up to and including the territorial waters of a state. When an aircraft transits international airspace through the ADIZ of a foreign state, the aircraft must do the following (abbreviated version):

(a) proceed without delay;

(b) refrain from any threat or use of force against the sovereignty, territorial integrity, or political independence of the foreign State; and

(c) follow other requirements for ships transiting through a strait.[97]

China's expanded ADIZ now stretches into the East China Sea, beyond Japan's designated EEZ "midpoint line" toward the Ryukyu Islands, and covers the contested Senkaku Islands. There is no question the new ADIZ covers a vast area of international airspace.

---

97 UNCLOS III, 1982; Paraphrased from Article 39.

The C-130 and P-3C Incidents

Two months after China announced the extension of its ADIZ, in January 2013, Chinese fighters followed a C-130 and a P-3A on separate occasions while both were peacefully transiting international airspace but in the new ADIZ. During both incidents the Chinese's fighters crossed over the Japan-China midpoint line.

The Attack on a US Reconnaissance Plane

There are two versions of the midair collision between the US E-P3 recon-naissance plane and the Chinese F-8 fighter. The collision took place approxi-mately sixty-four miles off the Chinese coast in international airspace, and all nations have a right of transit as delineated previously.

The collision took place in April 2001; in March 2003 I was given the Chinese version as taught to my undergraduate students by the Chinese Communist Party. Their version, which they all believed without question, was that the E-P3 attacked the F-8 Chinese fighter and intentionally rammed it, causing the death of their hero, the fighter pilot.

The second version as reported by the navy pilots was that the E-P3 was on autopilot, maintaining a constant altitude and airspeed, when the F-8 pilot proceeded to buzz the 130,000-pound, 105-foot-long E-P3, making passes within three feet of the E-P3. On his final pass, the F-8 pilot misjudged his maneuverability and hit one of the engines on the left wing.

It is possible the Chinese leadership did not intend to have its pilot hit the E-P3, but they had been made aware several months prior to this collision that its pilots had been maneuvering and harassing its reconnaissance airplanes for over three months. But once the accident occurred, the Chinese leadership took advantage of our newly sworn-in president and demanded and received most of their demands, notwithstanding the innocence and legal behavior of our US Navy pilots and crew.

The United States gave in to the Chinese to accomplish the new presi-dent's priority of the crew's safe return. The price was an apology made by the United States for an act it did not commit; the Chinese took every piece of equipment off the aircraft, and within a short period of time, they had reverse engineered our sensitive reconnaissance equipment; and our airplane had to be written off based on its destruction by the Chinese.

The United States provided the Chinese photographic evidence of their pilot's risky maneuvers, but the Chinese did not budge. Once again the United States was complying with all international laws, and the Chinese violated those same laws, but the United States lost significant face and vital national security hardware; the Chinese were given one more example of US leadership's tack of appeasing aggressors and international criminals.

CHAPTER 8

What to Do about China's and Russia's Territorial Goals That Conflict with US Interests

———

THERE IS A DIRECT CONNECTION between the financial and political health of the United States and the country's ability to help its allies fend off the Chinese in the South China Sea. For example the United States must be financially able to rebuild its armed forces so as to mount a credible threat to the Chinese, the Russians, and the Islamic terrorists at the same time. To do so the United States must first reverse the liberals' push toward socialism and isolationism.

Socialism and communism are alive and well in today's world, and past administrations used appeasement when confronted by both Russia and China; the American giant has for some time been ignoring and will probably continue into the foreseeable future to ignore the advances of these two governments and their goals of world domination.

The goals of these ideologies are the same now as they were in the mid-1900s. It is also true that the original concepts of Marx and Lenin were never achieved but were modified to fit the reality of human nature. The socialists and communists have intentionally modified their methods to achieve their goals in an attempt to ease infiltration into democratic and capitalistic societies. Russian leadership since 1991 has been attempting to portray its government as not following communist or socialist dogma but behind this façade it continues to allow the central government to expand its territory at the expense of free democratic countries.

The original intent of Marxism-Leninism was to have the communist philosophy voted into office using democratic systems so that the population would support the ideologies. Let us not forget that Adolf Hitler was voted into office using a legitimate democratic process. Trotsky proclaimed the method required to achieve world communism/socialism was revolution. During the period after Stalin's death in 1953, Mao Tse-tung supported revolution throughout many countries in the world until his death in 1976.

The background provided in this book was intended to convince readers of the dangerous path our nation has followed in dealing with the Chinese in the South China Sea and subsequently worldwide. There is no easy answer nor easy path to revive our country and once again be a leader among the nations of the world that support the idea humans are meant to be free—especially free from government control.

Left alone without government or prejudicial indoctrinations, prepubescent humans would develop naturally with an innate desire to be free and an ability to exercise and expand their capabilities to achieve happiness. Government must see that our citizens are not controlled by leaders who continually take more and more of our freedoms away and slowly destroy our will to enjoy a country where justice for all is a reality. Indeed, citizens can live in peace without fearing neighbors or the government, being free in our thoughts, and being allowed to pursue commerce without government interference.

Before any improvements can be made in executing an effective foreign policy, our nation must be reestablished economically, and America must counteract all government programs that lead to a socialist state. The following ideas are in no particular order, and all will be considered drastic by many. The alternative is to continue on the path we have followed as a nation, continually appeasing tyrants and tyrannical governments and allowing over half the country's population to be taken care of by the government with clothes, food, education, healthcare, and free phones at the expense of the population that produces, earns, creates, and pays taxes.

DOMESTIC AND FOREIGN POLICY

The foreign policy of the United States seems to be adrift at midocean with no one at the helm. Perhaps it is easier to understand that what is needed to protect our future is a better understanding of what does not work. The easiest way to understand how not to lead a country into socialism is to understand what government actions will create a path to socialism. Saul Alinsky in his *Rules for Radicals* provides an excellent list of tactics a government should implement to establish socialism. It is worth noting that Hillary Clinton wrote her dissertation on Alinsky, and President Obama has frequently noted he admires Alinsky so much he has been following his twelve precepts to the letter. Alinsky's Rules for Radicals, twelve in number, focus on tactics to use as a community organizer and government leaders intent on establishing a socialist country. The actual Alinsky's Rules were:

1. Power is not only what you have, but what the enemy thinks you have. Power is derived from 2 main sources – money and people. "Have-Nots" must build power from flesh and blood.
2. Never go outside the expertise of your people. It results in confusion, fear and retreat. Feeling secure adds to the backbone of anyone.
3. Whenever possible, go outside the expertise of the enemy. Look for ways to increase insecurity, anxiety and uncertainty.
4. Make the enemy live up to its own book of rules. If the rule is that every letter gets a reply, send 30,000 letters. You can kill them with this because no one can possibly obey all of their own rules.
5. Ridicule is man's most potent weapon. There is no defense. It's irrational. It's infuriating. It also works as a key pressure point to force the enemy into concessions.
6. A good tactic is one your people enjoy. They'll keep doing it without urging and come back to do more. They're doing their thing, and will even suggest better ones.
7. A tactic that drags on too long becomes a drag. Don't become old news.

8. Keep the pressure on. Never let up. Keep trying new things to keep the opposition off balance. As the opposition masters one approach, hit them from the flank with something new.

9. The threat is usually more terrifying than the thing itself. Imagination and ego can dream up many more consequences than any activist.

10. If you push a negative hard enough, it will push through and become a positive. Violence from the other side can win the public to your side because the public sympathizes with the underdog.

11. The price of a successful attack is a constructive alternative. Never let the enemy score points because you're caught without a solution to the problem.

12. Pick the target, freeze it, personalize it, and polarize it. Cut off the support network and isolate the target from sympathy. Go after people and not institutions; people hurt faster than institutions.[98]

The current administration seems to have defined Alinsky's "enemy" as the traditional American way of life. Contrary to propaganda being bantered freely about on the internet, Alinsky did not originate Eight Rules for converting a democracy to a socialist state. On the other hand, the following issues provide an excellent basis for discussing a possible strategy for reversing the US' slid towards socialism and its own destruction. Progressive politicians', such as Hillary Clinton, continually push the following socialist programs:

1. **Healthcare**—Control healthcare and you control the people.

2. **Poverty**—Increase the poverty level as high as possible; poor people are easier to control and will not fight back if you are providing everything for them to live.

3. **Debt**—Increase the debt to an unsustainable level. That way you are able to increase taxes, and this will produce more poverty.

4. **Gun Control**—Remove the ability to defend themselves from the government. That way you are able to create a police state.

---

98 Saul D. Alinsky, *Rules for Radicals: A Practical Primer for Realistic Radicals*, Random House, New York, 1971.

5. **Welfare**—Take control of every aspect of their lives (food, housing, and income).
6. **Education**—Take control of what people read and listen to—take control of what children learn in school.
7. **Religion**—Remove belief in G-d from the government and schools.
8. **Class Warfare**—Divide the people into the wealthy and the poor. This will cause more discontent, and it will be easier to tax the wealthy with the support of the poor.

Another interesting coincidence found in his book is that Alinsky was born in Chicago and educated first in the streets of that city and then in its university. It goes on to say the University of Chicago introduced him to the Capone gang. I am not sure what this means. Based on this section of his book, it appears his sole purpose in life was organizing and training leaders to use the poor to rebel against a government.

It is easy to draw a parallel between using the Alinsky's twelve rules and the above strategic targets when analyzing the current foreign and domestic policy of our government, which emphasizes that the citizens of the United States must once again be awakened as they were when Japan attacked Pearl Harbor. It is unrealistic to expect another catastrophic event to awaken the sleeping giant, so it must be done using our 230-year-old system of voting into office leaders who are willing to lead an extraordinary effort to undo deleterious advances along the lines of the above eight strategies and provide alternatives for our citizens. Our government must counter our march towards socialism which is the first step to returning our nation to its former greatness.

Healthcare

The Affordable Care Act is not the answer to our country's responsibility to provide healthcare for those who need and cannot afford it, but putting the federal government in charge of such a plan has and will continue to create more problems than it solves. One size does not fit all needs.

The drafters of the Constitution saw this when creating the Constitution to replace the Articles of Confederation. It applied in the 1700s and it applies today. Amassing so much power and control under one agency has never worked in business. Any businessperson elected to the presidency would take away the control from the federal agencies and allow each of our states and territories to set up their own systems. The federal government could have oversight authority over the sixty-six healthcare entities and perhaps smaller territories such as Bajo Nuevo Bank, Baker Island, and Howland Island, and these could be consolidated under one entity. The oversight would not provide instructions, guidance, or control of the healthcare entities but would be available when federal assistance was needed.

In business schools throughout the United States, span of control is studied and is generally based on how many tasks, based on complexity, one manager can handle. The average is twelve functions per manager, be they people, projects, or a combination of these. Assuming sixty healthcare entities for the United States, the federal government oversight should be limited to five managers with responsibility for approximately equal populations. And each would have a small supporting staff to collate and report on the needs of each entity. Simple, yes—and it works for business.

Each state and territory has its own healthcare challenges, and each must therefore design and manage its healthcare without interference from the federal government. By so doing, the federal government is deprived of its stranglehold on the healthcare of our needy population. For example, one or more entities present a problem to the federal oversight manager noting that the cost of drug *A* is limiting the number of patients who need drug *A* to survive. The federal department could then use established channels, either through the executive branch or Congress, to help solve the problem. The states would be free to continue their everyday management of their own healthcare systems and allow the federal government to address the issue of pricing with the appropriate branches of the federal government.

No longer would the federal government have control of the citizens; the states and territories would be their own health managers for the needy. If the citizens of each state or territory did not like or approve of their healthcare system, they have to right to change their government by voting them out of office in their own state or territory.

POVERTY

So goes the economy of the country, so goes the number of persons in poverty. Starting with the Progressive Party and Theodore Roosevelt, liberals of all kinds including the most influential, Karl Marx and Friedrich Engels (*The Communist Manifesto*) have advocated that the only way to solve poverty is to use government to artificially make everyone equal by taking away from the haves and giving it to the have-nots.

The problem is that a government that equalizes economic wealth artificially must, for eternity, guard against creeping wealth by some and a return to poverty by others. In other words, the government needs to be a single-party totalitarian entity in nature to prevent some from once again amassing wealth at the expense of others.

This century's liberals never discuss what happens if all citizens are economically equal and question who would lead the country if all citizens are forced to be equal. Would our leaders also be subject to forced equality? How does the country then choose its totalitarian leader(s)? Should they be chosen because they are more capable, and if so should they not be rewarded for their abilities as leaders? Oops—that would violate the equality rule.

For analysis, consider a government that was strong enough to force the wealthy to part with their gains so all citizens became economic equals. After this miracle, the government for some reason started losing its control over the economic distribution engine it created. For example, those running the engine wanted more and better food than the citizens they were serving and started lobbying against their own rules of economic distribution. Another issue would be how to control those with entrepreneurial skills from convincing others to give them some of their economic benefits.

Then there comes the issue of running industry to supply the nation with weapons to defend the country. Does any logically thinking person believe that the person capable of running a major facility would be happy earning exactly what a newly hired high school dropout would be paid? Enough written—taking from the rich and giving it to the poor only works to a certain point, and then the government finds itself in jeopardy from the talented leaders of industry who know how to organize and create.

Revolution would follow as sure as day follows night. Contrary to *The Communist Manifesto*, Alinsky, and liberal administrations, trying to take away wealth from some and giving it to the many will not work. There will always be inequality in life for biological and child development reasons. Accept it and live with this truth.

Once accepted, what can a nation do to solve the poverty issue? For sure we, as a nation, cannot let poverty kill off our citizens without helping. It is in our nature as humans to help those in need, so a system must be implemented to help, but not at the expense of bankrupting the country and destabilizing our economic system.

A proven economic system that works is for our government to reduce spending and implement business laws, regulations, and rules that provide for an ever-increasing output of our industries and economic success for all businesses. The biggest issue that needs to be addressed is the priorities of the federal government. Perhaps we, as a nation, cannot continue to put other countries ahead of ours when business decisions have to be made.

Also it seems we cannot afford to keep putting the continued existence of species such as the snail darter, *Percina tanasi*, ahead of our citizens in poverty. Yes, there is a connection between trying to do everything that is politically correct by attempting to control evolution of all species in our country at the expense of our citizens. All the funds expended on protecting endangered species could be used to reduce our deficit and help balance our budget.

True, many citizens, but probably not a majority, would never agree to the above fiscal policy. But as soon as those citizens are given a choice between providing a decent education, living conditions, and healthcare for a poverty-stricken family, then what or whom would they choose?

Another tough issue is whether to have physically capable individuals receiving government funds work for those funds. Franklin Roosevelt did it and it worked. But before our government can afford public works–type projects, it must balance the budget and entitlements. No, I am not an economist, but using simple logic, tough decisions have to be made that any business-person would make to protect our country from the Alinsky and *Communist Manifesto* predictions that class struggles are the way to socialize a government. If we continue to have over half our population depending on government for all their needs and less than half working to earn money to pay for these entitlements, then the Alinsky/communist predictions will come true, and our country will become a nation in revolt.

Debt and Economic Boycott of China

The largest ship in the world carries eighteen thousand containers and steams between China and the United States. It brings these containers full of Chinese merchandise and goes back almost empty from our country. This is just one description of the imbalance in trade between our country and China. Our trade imbalance with China for 2015 has been estimated at $530 billion with imports from China at $2,230 billion. Should the US government interfere with this trade the loss of money would devastate China. True, the United States also depends on China as a receiver of our imports—in 2015 the total amount of merchandise sold to China was approximately $2,761 billion, which represents a large number of businesses and jobs. Notwithstanding the impact on our economy, some form of economic boycott of Chinese goods would be preferable to war.

In order to balance the equation, the United States would have to tax Chinese goods entering our country at approximately 19.2 percent. These numbers are based on the 2015 imbalance in trade. Translated into reality means a $1.00 toy bought at Walmart would be $1.20. Naturally the Chinese products would no longer be as attractive as they are at today's prices, so fewer sales means less import over time. Also one would expect retaliation, with China imposing its own tariff so the war would be limited to commerce.

A less drastic and probably more effective method would be to start at a 2 percent tariff and continue to add 1 percent each year until the trade imbalance is ameliorated. The carrot for China would be to open its purse and start buying American. They could, for example, stop stealing our aircraft designs and just buy our commercial aircraft—just a thought.

The Chinese continue to buy American real estate and businesses with the imbalanced profits, and our leaders do nothing. Perhaps our government needs to start thinking about protecting the United States and use economics to get the Chinese to back off in the South China Sea and in their economic attacks against us.

GUN CONTROL

The Second Amendment contains two parts and must be read and interpreted together:

Part 1: A well-regulated Militia, being necessary to the security of a free State...
Part 2: the right of the people to keep and bear Arms, shall not be infringed.

As the thirteen colonies wanted a bill of rights added to the Constitution so as to maintain their status as a state in the newly formed federation, Pennsylvania had its own bill of rights, which read as follows:

Section 13—Declaration of Rights: That the people have a right to bear arms for the defense of themselves and the state; and as standing armies in the time of peace are dangerous to liberty, they ought not to be kept up; and that the military should be kept under strict subordination to, and governed by, the civil power.

The Federalists and Antifederalists were firm believers that tyranny under the Constitution was not possible because the people were armed. All the states had some form of declaration of rights showing an understanding that the people of America should possess arms in order to preserve liberty and protect themselves against tyranny, and tyranny was and is defined is that which il-legitimates political regimes.

Progressive politicians realized that when socialism started to deprive Americans of freedom, the giant would awaken and, if armed, would make it difficult, perhaps impossible, for a communist/socialist form of government to exist. Rhetoric intended to overshadow the real reason certain progressive politicians and their followers want to eviscerate the Second Amendment goes something like this:

> Gun control ends gun violence as surely an antibiotics end bacterial infections, as surely as vaccines end childhood measles—not perfectly and in every case, but overwhelmingly and everywhere that it's been taken seriously and tried at length. These lives can be saved. Kids continue to die *en masse* because one political party won't allow that to change, and the party won't allow it to change because of the *irrational and often paranoid fixations* that make the massacre of students and children an acceptable cost of fetishizing guns.[99]

Australia is generally held up as a shining example that gun control works. From 1979 to 1996 there were thirteen mass shootings in Australia, and after 1996 there have been none. After the Port Arthur massacre in Tasmania, the Australian government passed gun control measures banning automatic and semiautomatic weapons.

Gun control supporters go on to compare Australia's murder and robbery rates with those in the United States but fail to analyze the population density of each country. Australia has 2.66 persons per square kilometer; the United States has 31.27 persons for the same area. One can also compare HIV/AIDS deaths: seventeen thousand (2012 estimated) in Australia versus fewer than one hundred (2009 estimated) for the United States in 2009. Perhaps less populous density has an effect on mass murders. The point is that Australia and the United States are vastly different when it comes to mass psychology,

---

99   Adam Gopnik, "The Second Amendment Is a Gun-Control Amendment," *The New Yorker*, October 2, 2015.

behavior, human nature, and so forth, so one data point on a graph does not provide a defined solution to a problem.

The Second Amendment was meant to protect citizens from a tyrannical government, notwithstanding certain politicians, including President Obama, stating that tyranny is a myth and will never happen in the United States. Then one questions the logic in our chief executive fighting so hard to implement the above eight programs for establishing socialism. Therefore, the corollary is to reverse the trend and apply common sense to gun control legislation so our citizens can defend themselves and protect themselves and their state.

WELFARE

There is a marked difference between welfare and socialism. Welfare is institutionalized aid to citizens who cannot care for themselves or do not have family to protect their health and existence; some form of welfare is a must for all civilized societies. Socialism, on the other hand, is a government becoming the parent and responsible adult for citizens who are capable of taking care of themselves.

Numbers and statistics can be manipulated to support vastly different causes and effects; the following statistics are provided to help identify the effectiveness of the current administration's plan to implement one of the progressive political targets:

2012—150,026,000 people getting some type of federal benefit other than veterans' benefits; 82,679,000 people on Medicaid; 51,471,000 households on food stamps; 22,526,000 on Women, Infants, and Children program; 20,355,000 on Supplemental Security Income; 13,267,000 lived in public housing or got housing subsidies; 5,442,000 got temporary assistance to needy families; and 4,517,000 received other forms of federal cash assistance. The total population of the United States at the end of 2012 was estimated at 314,100,000. These numbers cannot be compared in a meaningful way because of the variety of permutations and combinations possible, so it will not be tried. The poverty guideline for a family of three is approximately $20,000 (full-time work at $10.60 per hour).

By themselves the previous estimates on citizens receiving socialized financial aid are meaningless, but the number must be reduced to provide more funds for national defense. As the US budget is today, it is necessary to continue using credit (debt) to pay for welfare entitlements and military defense. Budget decisions for the last decade have favored entitlements and not the military; the American giant cannot defend our country without a strong military. The socialist economic system will not allow for funding our military to the levels needed to force China to back off from its goal of world domination starting with the South China Sea. Therefore, the connection between progressive politicians' target on taking control of every aspect of citizens' lives must be reversed and a capitalistic free-market enterprise be reinstated.

EDUCATION

Education is not restricted to schools. It also includes mass media and control of what citizens read, listen to, and watch. It starts with educating our young to accept communism/socialism before they reach puberty. The Chinese are masters at this as noted previously.

The United States must reinstate education without political bias. John Stuart Mill carefully and with emphasis explained the inherent problems with government schools. "A general state education is a mere contrivance for molding people to be exactly like one another, and as the mold in which it casts them is that which pleases the predominant power in government... it establishes a despotism over the mind, leading by natural tendency to one over the body," he wrote.

The Constitution did not place education of our young under the wing of the federal government; the founders of our country wanted the states to control education. President Harding was the first to envision the federal government taking a role in education, and President Eisenhower actually approved the formation of the Department of Health, Education and Welfare. In 1979 the Department of Education (under President Carter) was separated from Health and Welfare.

There seems to be no question the states were intended to be the caretakers of education, and nothing prevented the federal government from exercising oversight responsibilities. The federal government is now forcing all states to adopt the Common Core Standards, which have not been received well by educators. The one complaint about Common Core that affects the South China Sea is that readings of historic classical works have been removed from curricula and replaced with writing reflecting government-style documents and the distortion of Common Core English, which is not politically correct. Many pundits have described Common Core as having an anti-free-market enterprise, prosocialism, and proliberal agenda.

President Obama and his liberal appointees, being afraid of professional educators not accepting Common Core, have made a $4.35 billion Department of Education program called Race to the Top. The use of these funds is dependent on each state's acceptance of Common Core—it is a bribe by the Obama administration to get states to accept a program that is counter to nonbiased education.

To curb the Clinton-Obama agenda of molding our young in the form of future liberals, states must be given back the power to control their own school curricula and standards. An alternative is for the federal government to recommend that states provide a well-balanced education based on the current and future realities founded in our Constitution and Bill of Rights.

All school systems need to target children under twelve and thirteen years of age with basic patriotism and love for the American way of life. Once these children reach maturity and have ingrained patriotic feelings for the United States, then liberals who put foreign nations' interests before ours will be out of favor and influence. Putting America first and waking our giant will be necessary to protect us, our allies, and the world from China's continued aggression and creeping socialism.

The US Congress and executive branch of our government must be aware that as long as the People's Republic of China remains a single-party, totalitarian communist/socialist government, its goals of world domination will not change. In free societies, each generation changes depending on its freedom to explore new ideas and concepts of living and being governed. China has instituted education and censorship as weapons of domination.

One major technique used by totalitarian governments to overcome the natural human desire for life, liberty, and happiness is indoctrination from an early age. Child development psychologists agree that human value systems and behaviors are generally set by puberty, with the child's initial understanding of cultural norms and behaviors being established by the age of six. Between six and puberty, children tend to test their value/behavior norms and adapt as necessary to please their role models. After puberty, developmental psychologists seem to agree that changing value, belief, and behavioral systems in humans is very difficult.

People function best when they are recognized for their accomplishments, have status in society, and consistently achieve their goals. A totalitarian government that wants to ensure society does *not* constantly attempt to pursue life, liberty, and happiness must therefore overcome the basic nature of the humans in its society. The use of force tends to fail as an instrument of change of human nature. At best, force only modifies behavior to conform to an acceptable norm set by a totalitarian government. Therefore, indoctrination at an early age is best. China is a master at indoctrinating its young before puberty and thereby ensuring continued support of the Chinese Communist Party.

My undergraduate students in China did not believe me when I described American lifestyles. For example, when I described traveling from Santa Monica, California, to Jacksonville, Florida, on a freeway with no tolls, red lights, detours, or trash deposits, and few billboards, they believed I had been brainwashed by the government, or I was lying about the Eisenhower freeway system (our interstate highways).

Slowly I formed the opinion that these college students had been thoroughly indoctrinated by the Chinese education system to believe only information provided by the party, and they were not open to new ideas. As a visiting professor, I was prohibited from discussing Tibet, Korea, the South

China Sea, the Chinese Communist Party, the Tiananmen Square massacre, the economic conditions of Russia and China, and so forth.

History provided by undergraduate universities completely ignores the tens of millions of people who died of starvation during Mao Tse-tung's policy of rapid industrialization and collectivization of land, the Great Leap Forward. They were aware, on the other hand, that Deng Xiao-ping eventually implemented needed reforms in the economic sector of China by allowing some growth of capitalism.

None of the undergraduate students who were brave enough to talk to me knew that over one hundred thousand people had gathered in Beijing with the intent of overthrowing the ruling elite, and the only government act that saved the Communist Party was that, during the night of June 3 and the early hours of June 4, Chinese troops beat, bayoneted, and shot protesters. Tanks drove straight into crowds, crushing people and bicycles under their treads. By 6:00 a.m. on June 4, the streets around Tiananmen Square had been cleared.

Keep in mind all Chinese military forces answer to the Communist Party and not to the citizens of China. The military has to swear an oath to support the party—not the country. Visualize, if you will, all American armed forces swearing allegiance to the Democratic Party and not the Constitution.

I was invited to visit a grade school and was greeted by elementary-grade children wearing red scarfs identifying them as members of the Young Pioneers of China (ages six to fourteen), which was run by the Communist Youth League. I was asked by these children why the United States was lying about Tiananmen Square and saying bad things about the heroes from the June 4, 1989, incident. They honestly believed it was Western ideology that caused the death of the 250 to 7,000 humans massacred. (The children did not know the numbers, but they had a sense of the severity of the issue.)

The Soviet Union realized within one generation that pure communism and socialism would never work economically. Had humans been a homogeneous species without individual thought, perhaps the concept may have worked. For example, if one studies an ant colony, one may conclude that communism works perfectly for the ants. This line of reasoning would also work for animals that swarm with decisions being made by the collective will of the members of the group.

The same philosophy would seem to apply to herds of animals where each individual animal by itself cannot make good decisions, but as a herd, they seem to survive better and make more reasonable life-protecting decisions. The difficulty for communism and socialism is that humans work better when individuals are allowed to think for themselves. The herd mentality when applied to humans does not work, as evidenced by normal, peace-loving, indigenous populations such as Germans in the late 1930s making unreasonable collective decisions supporting genocide and atrocities that individuals would probably not have done.

Also a problem for pure communism and socialism is that humans tend to perform more efficiently when led rather than being pushed. One of the greatest experiments supporting this concept was at the AT&T Western Electric Hawthorne Plant in Cicero, Illinois, between 1924 and 1932. The purpose of the experiments was to determine how best to improve the productivity of workers to maximize profit. Two of the experiments stand out and are useful for discussing the economic failures of communism and socialism.

The first experiment dealt with improving working conditions for the workers to see what effects increased lighting, seating arrangements, bench organization, and other miscellaneous changes had on production output. The workers used for the experiment were assembling relays, and the results showed improvement in efficiency every time the working condition was improved. The team conducting the experiments was surprised when the experimental workstation improvements were taken away from the workers and the efficiency of the workers improved or at least remained at the highest peak obtained during the experiment. The analysis used at the time was referred to as the "observer effect," which suggested that the basis for the improvement in efficiency was that the workers were being observed rather than the actual change in conditions.

A similar experiment was conducted using monetary rewards to determine the impact on efficiency, and much to the surprise of the examiners, efficiency decreased. These experiments were important bases for work by later behavioral psychologists such as Dr. Frederick Herzberg, who identified conditions under which humans achieve the highest degree of effectiveness and happiness.

Simply stated, Dr. Herzberg distinguished between "motivators" and "hygiene factors." The conclusion based on years of research and experimentation defines the ideal situation as one in which humans are highly motivated and have few complaints when they are challenged by their work, recognized for their accomplishments, and given responsibility for their own behavior and efficiency. These factors are internalized by humans, and the hygiene factors of status, job security, salary, fringe benefits, and working conditions do not motivate humans, but without these factors, humans become dissatisfied with their lives.

Now compare this with socialism, where one centralized, single-party government takes care of all human needs under socialist control; without basic motivators, humans will eventually become dissatisfied with socialism. How about communism where no one has status, responsibility, or leadership—where Tom has two potatoes, John has one potato, and Steve has no potatoes, then Tom must give one of his potatoes to Steve. And if he does not give up his excess, the government will take it away and give it to Steve. Perhaps this concept is analogous to politicians, starting with President Franklin Delano Roosevelt, believing that the government needs to take away from the rich and give it to the poor.

The former Soviet Union (now Russia), China, North Korea, Vietnam, Cuba, and all other communist/socialist countries created and maintain single-party dictatorial forms of government, denying their citizens the opportunity to achieve the conditions necessary for happiness, freedom, and work environments that lead to prosperity and personal growth of each human. The economic systems of these countries have all failed.

China's Deng Xiao-ping was the first leader to realize capitalism was necessary for his country to progress economically, using phrases often quoted such as these:

* Let some people get rich first.
* When our thousands of Chinese students abroad return home, you will see how China will transform itself.
* To get rich is glorious.
* Poverty is not socialism. To be rich is glorious.

Xi Jin-ping, a leader of China, appears to be nervous about integrating Marxism with capitalism; the Associated Press reported on December 30, 2014, that China needed to ensure that higher-learning institutions were a fundamental guarantee for running socialist universities with Chinese features. Xi tightened controls on artists, churches, and others and ordered reporters to undergo training in Marxism to emphasize the ruling party's dominance. Marxism, remember, is based on class struggle leading to revolution, the dictatorship of the proletariat, and eventual development of a classless society with capitalism superseded by socialism.

Biophysics supports the opinion that for a communistic system to succeed and become self-reproductive requires substantial amounts of energy. The purpose of this external energy is to overcome millenniums of human development and the creation of a new DNA and gene pool. When humans are left alone to develop on their own without government interference, they tend to want to survive and reproduce. Reproduction, according to Darwinian models, tends to produce new generations with improved survivability characteristics. There is no genetic marker that supports the communist-socialist system of political organization.

With humans having developed as hunter-gatherers with strong survival instincts, having a central government take care of the individuals was counterproductive. The ability to move around to take advantage of different climates and conditions on earth seemed to provide for the basic five elements of survival. If humans are left alone to survive, they do not select a communist or socialist system for survival—they become more independent and rely more on themselves, which is evident in the first motivational concepts pushing humans toward recognition, achievement, and status. These basic elements were used to help the human race survive and generally created a genetic disposition toward being free.

To overcome these basic instincts in humans, when they are born, requires a significant amount of external energy forcing changes in survival instincts. The only thing the communist single-party system provides is the external energy to force humans to accept extinction or adaptation to the forced system of communism-socialism.

This is evident even in an almost purely communistic totalitarian state such as China, where there are occasional uprisings of its citizens to fight the system. When human nature takes over, it takes an extreme amount of pressure, such as the 1989 Tiananmen Square massacre, to force humans back into line. Since humans are reproducing all the time, they tend to create more freedom-loving humans than their competitor communists and socialists. Therefore, for the communist and socialist system to survive, it must force using education at a very early age as previously explained and have the power to control the behavior of the citizens.

RELIGION

Benjamin Franklin was an agnostic, but he did believe religion was necessary for the human race. His logic was based on the volatility of human nature and the ability of most religions to calm the savage beast lying in wait in the human soul. Science has proven that humans can be easily programmed to harm animals and other humans. An extreme example is Hitler's and his henchmen's ability to convince humans to exterminate a segment of the world's population based on religion.

Progressive politicians require removal of religion from schools and government; by so doing, society has opened our young, impressionable minds to communist/socialist doctrines and belief since they are not religious in nature. Without religious teachings, our young have no defense against radical thoughts. Think of today's college campuses where hooligans who do not like what a speaker stands for will cause riots to stifle his or her speech notwithstanding the First Amendment.

It is easy to recognize the Obama administration's attempts to eliminate G-d from our educational institutions. Students are punished for exhibiting any form of acknowledgment of a deity, and schools must remove all signs of religion from their campuses. Religions have always influenced the development of children, especially their value systems. Their formative years are between birth and puberty, after which it is difficult to change them.

This technique was discussed in this book earlier in reference to the Chinese shaping children's value systems before puberty. The Chinese young are susceptible because the Communist Party of China has eliminated all religions from its education and civil communities. The few surviving remnants of religious pockets in China are severely restricted on seeking converts.

To combat China and its world conversion goal, the United States must truly allow freedom of religion in all institutions and not allow a few atheists to stifle our freedom and exercise our beliefs without fear of government intervention. If the progressive agenda concerning religion is not reversed, it is possible our nation will develop along the lines of other nations that only allow a government-approved religion and stone to death believers of a god not of the government's choice.

President Obama, following the progressive agenda to remove religion from education, had his advanced team insist on the shrouding of all vestiges of religion before he would agree to speak at Notre Dame and Georgetown University.

CLASS WARFARE

For the last thirty-five years, 324,000 blacks have been killed by blacks. Ninety percent of blacks were murdered by blacks (single victim/single shooter) and 10 percent of blacks were killed by whites. Yet for years the Obama administration has focused its attorney general on targeting police forces around the United States anytime a black person is killed by a white police officer. Every time there is a mass shooting, the Obama administration increases pressure on gun control.

On March 16, 2016, Paul Joseph Watson's headlines read: *"TOP BLACK LIVES MATTER ACTIVIST: 'WE WILL INCITE RIOTS EVERYWHERE IF TRUMP WINS,'"* quoting activist and rapper Tef Poe giving a message to "white people." At the end of seven years of Obama's leadership, the United States is more divided by class than it was in 1964. When groups want to equalize economic levels, the administration pressures Congress to raise taxes on the wealthy and give more tax dollars to entitlement programs. When a white officer kills a black person, no matter what the circumstances, the Obama administration but nothing is reported by the White House if a black police officer kills a white suspect or when a white police officer wrongfully kills another white.

A constant barrage of newspaper articles, White House press conferences, statements by the president, and riots and uprisings led by groups such as Black Lives Matter, Black Panthers, and white supremacy groups continually stir the class-warfare pot, reinforcing the progressive agenda and divides people into classes that will cause discontent and revolution.

Poor citizens are created by poor economic conditions, and more poor citizens create another class distinction—the haves and have-nots. Marx and Lenin depended on the two class divisions to create warfare between the classes. As noted before, China did not have class divisions to help start a revolution, so Mao Tse-tung had to use other excuses.

But, today, in the United States, it seems that our government has been increasing the divide between classes by race and economics in accordance with progressive politicians' goal 8—class warfare. Alinsky went on to state that by so doing it would be easier to tax the wealthy with the support of the poor. The poor, of course, are being supported by welfare provided by the government in accordance with his Rule 5 and by healthcare according to target 1, and more poverty is created in keeping with the progressive politicians' goal 2, which provides an ever-increasing movement toward the destruction of the US democratic, free-market economy. And it follows naturally that the government's debt will increase as required by prgressive politicians' goal 3, which adds to our march toward socialism.

APPEASEMENT

Since the Chinese attacked and killed fifty-three Vietnamese, injured sixteen, and captured forty-eight (including one American advisor) in 1974, the United States either has attempted to appease the Chinese or our politicians have made protest noises with no intention of following up with action. It has not worked. Appeasement continues with no action.

Steaming our ships close to disputed formations in the South China Sea does not now nor ever will intimidate the Chinese. They continue to fortify formations with expanded radars and armaments. The United States does nothing. We continue to let our allies go it alone like we did when asked to help the Vietnamese defend the Paracel Islands. Our response was that no help would be given because the Chinese invasion and the Vietnamese attempt to oust the intruders was merely "a local matter."

ISOLATIONISM

Isolationism is always an option but not a viable one. The enemies of the United States are now coming to America. They sneak in physically; they cyber-attack us, they come across our borders with impunity, and they are taking over our economic engines in the form of real estate and formerly American-owned corporations.

Shutting our eyes and ears to the world around us will not work; two major world forces are our sworn enemies and are intent on destroying America: communism/socialism and radical Islam, intent on carrying out the dictates of the Koran specifying Sharia law above all others. The question then becomes how are Judge Carolyn Walker-Diallo and Rep. Keith Ellison (D-MN) going to uphold the Constitution of the United States when they swore their oath of office on the Koran? Our leaders, such as President Obama and the majority of his political appointees seem to believe in appeasing every nation but the United States; in our country they have and will probably continue to follow the tenets and the objectives of the progressive politicians.

MILITARY INTERVENTION

We must be ready for war so as to prevent war. We are not ready. In 1978 there were fifteen active-duty fleet carriers available for service in the US Navy—today there are only ten. Yes, the fleet carriers of today can carry a few more planes and are electronically superior to the carriers of my day, but they are still limited in number and cannot be in more than one hostile part of the world at a time. Each of our guided-missile destroyers is better armed than those of the sixties, seventies, and eighties, yet again they are limited in numbers.

On the other hand, when the navy decides to build a light, fast, well-armed multimission ship, the administration cuts the standing order from fifty-two ships to forty and only commits to building six between fiscal years 2017 and 2020. For sailors who need fast shallow-water-capable multipurpose ships today, 2020 is a long ways away.

Other marine, army, air force, and coast guard experts can provide examples of the cuts to their services thanks to a government focused on becoming more socialist in place of building a strong defense to protect us.

CHAPTER 9

The Big Picture in the South China Sea

———

THE FIRST SECTION OF THIS book provided a synopsis of Chinese history and its progress to spread communism and socialism throughout the world. Putting all China's aggressive wars in one list has the purpose of convincing readers that China cannot be trusted as long as it has a single-party system of government and while its military force pledges allegiance to the Communist Party and not the people, or until the citizens of China are not afraid to teach their children about being free of government control and allow them to pursue happiness and experience free-market enterprises.

The second section provided a short guide on how ocean formations are acquired by nations under international law and UNCLOS III as guides. Several examples of Chinese aggressive behavior and violations of accepted international law highlight what an impartial tribunal would decide if the conflicts were placed before it.

Finally, I discussed some ideas on how to repair the damage to the United States inflicted on us by our appeasement-oriented series of government leaders and socialist-leaning politicians. The recommendations are few because the one not addressed is eventually that the United States must stand up to the bully in the South China Sea, and to do this the nation needs to rebuild its military arm so we may strike anywhere in the world against nations that attempt to take away our freedom of the seas and our constitutional rights within our borders.

An Abraham Lincoln quote is as appropriate today as it was during his tenure as president: "My dream is of a place and a time where America will once again be seen as the last hope of earth."

To accomplish President Lincoln's dream, our elected representatives, congressmen, senators, and presidents must make decisions that are best for the nation and not what citizens are demanding, and they definitely must not appoint an executive branch based on repaying debts to friends and campaign contributors. Doing what is best for the nation will cause many honorable citizens to loudly complain and argue against decisions that are best for America. But our government push toward socialism must be stopped, and there will be national pain and unrest during the process.

The alternative is unthinkable, and it would make President John Adams's quote burn in the memories of all who would live under a socialist government: "Remember, democracy never lasts long. It soon wastes, exhausts, and murders itself. There never was a democracy yet that did not commit suicide."

Let our nation not commit suicide by allowing our government to continue implementing the progressive politician's eight targets. By reversing the process, our nation will be great again—first economically, after which the American giant will return to being true to Lincoln's dream.

About the Author

———

JAMES M. FONES II HAS been traveling the world for his entire life. During his formative years, he climbed Ancon Hill, Panama, to watch ships transiting the canal and lived in Guatemala during the revolutionary years before joining the US Navy at seventeen. As an enlisted man for five years and an officer for nineteen, he learned to perfect his English and commence his education. He graduated from the Armed Forces Staff College and was posted to the American embassy in Caracas, Venezuela, and was the aide and translator for the chief of naval operations of Bolivia for the Sixth Inter-American Naval Conference. During his tour in Vietnam, serving as an advisor on a Vietnamese gunboat, he received two Crosses of Gallantry and was awarded the Bronze Star for action defending a village on the Basac River. After retiring as a commander, he completed a bachelor of science in law (summa cum laude) and a juris doctorate. He practiced immigration, bankruptcy, and family law in California for twelve years and was selected as a pro tem judge for five years.

Fones then became the general manager of a shipyard in Pago Pago, American Samoa, working with ship owners from various countries in the South Pacific. He later spent five years as a visiting professor for two universities in China and provided consulting services to a major Shanghai law firm. During his time in China, he completed his post doctorate (Legum Magister) in international law and commenced his research on legal issues surrounding the China's forceful acquisition of ocean formations in the South China Sea.

Simultaneously Fones commenced study of the United States and its inability to support its allies in Asia and its continued march toward socialism.

During his military and civilian careers, Fones became aware of the United States losing it world credibility and inability to protect weaker countries from the world domination goals of China and Russia